SEARCH THE SCRIPTURES

SEARCH THE SCRIPTURES

Volume 2

Leviticus - Ruth

by

Cornelis VanderWaal

PAIDEIA PRESS
St. Catharines, Ontario, Canada

Most of this material was originally published in Dutch under the title *Sola Scriptura*, © Oosterbaan & Le Cointre N.V. of Goes. Translated by Theodore Plantinga.

 Published by Paideia Press, P.O. Box 1450, St. Catharines, Ontario, Canada, L2R 7J8.

Bible quotations are taken from the Revised Standard Version unless otherwise indicated.

ISBN 0-88815-022-9
Printed in the United States of America.

Table of Contents

LEVITICUS

NUMBERS

DEUTERONOMY

JOSHUA

JUDGES

RUTH

Leviticus

You shall be holy to me; for I the
LORD am holy (20:26).

1. Laws for a Holy Nation

The Mosaic laws. There is a story about Gandhi, the famous Indian leader, that sheds some light on our attitudes toward the Bible. While he was studying in London, Gandhi decided to read the Bible. He found Genesis and Exodus, the first two books, very exciting, but Leviticus put him to sleep. Not until the Gospel according to Matthew and the Sermon on the Mount did he find anything else that held his attention.

In our discussion of the Bible, we have now reached the point where Gandhi's interest in the Book of books began to wane. Professing Christians often show little more interest in all the Mosaic legislation than Gandhi did. Yet, if we hope to attain a proper understanding of the message of the Bible, we must work our way through those laws. We must do so first of all because the entire Bible is God's Word and demands our attention. Secondly, the gospel of

Christ is also revealed in the laws of Moses. The fact that the Letter to the Hebrews cannot be properly understood without a knowledge of the book of Leviticus illustrates this.

In the laws about sacrifices and in the regulations for priests and festivals, we hear the joyful message of the One who was to fulfill all the requirements better than any priest of the tribe of Levi could ever do. Therefore we must do our best to get a concrete picture of the practices we read about and to understand their meaning. Of course we cannot go into every detail. All the same, it is very important that certain central points be brought to the fore.

The main idea. First of all, let's look at the *content* of the book of Leviticus. Chapters 1-7 deal with offerings and 8-10 with regulations for beginning the services in the tabernacle. Chapters 11-15 contain laws about purity and impurity, followed by rules for the great Day of Atonement (ch. 16). Finally, there are more laws, this time about "holiness" (ch. 17-26), as well as some stipulations about vows (ch. 27).

There is a *theme* binding all these laws and stipulations together. We find it in 20:26: "You shall be *holy* to me; for I the LORD am holy, and have separated you from the peoples, that you should be *mine*." This is a statement of the main idea governing the entire book of Leviticus. This theme reminds us again of what we identified as the central theme of the five books of Moses as a whole: "You shall be to me a kingdom of priests and a *holy* nation" (Ex. 19:6).

A nation set apart. Israel was a *holy* nation. This does not mean—as we might be inclined to think, under the influence of a Roman Catholic conception of holiness—that Israel was somehow a sinless nation. If you have read the history of Israel, you know better. No, *holy* means *set apart* for the service of the Lord.

Israel, as a holy nation, was claimed completely by the

Lord for His purposes. The day-to-day affairs of the Israelites, their liturgy, their sexual life—in short, all they did was to be viewed in the light of His covenantal admonition: "Be holy, for I am holy" (see I Pet. 1:16).

Descending to Israel's level. We must not forget that Israel was still a "child" and was still in need of considerable guidance and training. Israel's thoughts moved on a level comparable to that of the primitive peoples of our time. Therefore the Lord had to speak in language understandable to Israel when He revealed Himself.

Scholars have pointed out that the laws of Moses include many regulations that are to be found in the legislation of other nations as well. This is not to be denied. The Lord definitely descended to Israel's level, to its intellectual climate and limitations. But on the other hand, we must not make the mistake of thinking that the "law" was binding for Israel because it reflected *Israel's* sense of the divine; it was binding because it came from *the Lord,* the God of the covenant.

The uniqueness of Israel's laws. On many points there are significant *differences* between the laws given to the Israelites and the practices and regulations of the pagans in the ancient Near East. To take one example, the pagans attached great significance to the power of *blood*. We have already seen that blood played a great role in Israel's laws as well. But the pagans were inclined to reason as follows: if blood is the seat of life, we should *drink* the blood of sacrificed animals in order to partake of the life of the gods.

Leviticus *opposes* this line of reasoning. Blood is given by the Lord as a means of atonement. Therefore it is never to be consumed (see 3:17; 7:26; 17:10, 14; see also Gen. 9:4; Acts 15:20, 29). When a sacrifice was made, the blood was to be poured at the foot of the altar, for it belonged to the Lord. Here we have a typical *anti-heathen* law.

I can give you another example. Among the heathens, the king was often considered a son of the gods and therefore served as high priest. This was not allowed in Israel. Furthermore, Israel's priests were not a class of enchanters elevated far above the people because of some secret ritual. No, just as the king in later Israel was simply a man of the people and is described for us in the Bible with all his faults, Israel's priests were simply instruments in the hand of Yahweh to mediate between Him and His people. There was no secret teaching or any hocus-pocus involved. The priests were to teach the people the law.

We should likewise note that the person bringing the offering was himself involved in the service of sacrifice, for example, by laying his hand on the head of the animal. Moreover, Leviticus does not hide the fact that the tribe of Levi was subject to the same pitfalls as the other tribes. At the very first service of sacrifice conducted by Aaron and his sons, things already went wrong: Nadab and Abihu broke the Lord's regulations as they brought fire to the altar and were immediately consumed by the Lord's holiness (10:1-2). The weakness of the priesthood of Levi's order was apparent from the very beginning.

The imperfection of this order of priests was made especially clear on the great Day of Atonement. On that day, which came once a year, the high priest sprinkled blood not only because of the sins of the people but also because of the liturgical transgressions he and his relatives had committed during the preceding year. Scripture was making it painfully clear that some day another Priest would have to replace these priests. Levi's service was only provisional.

Here we see what is unique about the sacrificial customs of the Israelites. The offering of a sacrifice did not mean that man was elevating himself by being so gracious as to give his god a gift. Rather, in this cultic activity the Lord was approaching His people by showing them a path that would lead to the reconciliation and communion with Him.

2. The Offerings Prescribed by the Lord

A thorough knowledge of God's revelation. Because we repeatedly come across offerings of various sorts as we read the Old Testament, we should know something about the different types of offerings. Now, you might feel inclined to excuse yourself on this score by pointing out that the average Bible reader knows very little about this matter. What you say is true, of course, but it still remains *your* task to gain a thorough knowledge of God's revelation, which includes the different kinds of offerings. What others know and do not know cannot serve as a norm for you. All too often, we church people play idle games with the riches entrusted to us.

Here is a short survey of the types of offerings. First of all, there are two major types to be distinguished: (1) freewill offerings, (2) sin offerings and guilt offerings. We will begin by considering the kinds of freewill offerings.

Burnt offerings. One kind of freewill offering is the burnt offering (1:17). Someone who proposed to make such an offering could choose between three possibilities: he could offer a young bull, an unblemished male sheep or goat, or doves or pigeons (the offering of the poor man).

This offering clearly reflected consecration to the Lord. The person bringing the offering would place his hand on the head of the animal being sacrificed. This signified that the sacrificial animal was taking the place of the person, in accordance with the law of substitution. The life of the animal took the place of the life or soul of the person. Actually, *human* blood would have to flow in order to atone for sin, but for the present the Lord would allow the blood of animals to take the place of human blood.

First the person bringing the offering kills the animal. Then comes the "manipulation of the blood," something that requires our special attention. The priests catch the blood of the slain animal as it drains out of the body and sprinkle it on the great altar of burnt offering, which stands in the court of the tabernacle.

Through this action, the blood, as the seat of the "soul" or of life, is offered to the Lord. Thereby the sin is atoned for and covered in God's sight. The blood *in itself* is of no significance—we are not dealing here with a form of magic revolving around blood—but the Lord accepts the blood of the sacrificial animal as a replacement for the life of the person bringing the offering.

The person bringing the offering then skins the animal, cutting it into pieces just as if he were preparing a meal. *With his own hands*, he symbolically carries out the judgment on himself. You recall that at an earlier point in the ceremony, he gives expression to his oneness with the animal by laying his hand on its head.

After this part of the ceremony, the priests enter the picture again. They place everything on the altar and present it to Yahweh. They wash the unclean entrails and legs with water, for the offering must be clean. Then they start the fire, and the burnt offering rises to the Lord in the form of a pleasing odor, an odor that *brings rest*. (The latter phrase represents a more accurate translation of the Hebrew.) You recall that Noah's sacrifice after the flood also brought "rest." In fact, the name *Noah* means *rest*.

The offering brings rest, comfort, reconciliation. We are not to assume, as the Canaanites did, that God takes an actual sensual pleasure in odors. But the Lord does accept the offering; it meets with His approval.

Meal offerings. Another kind of freewill offering is the meal offering (2:1-16). This offering is also spoken of as a "memorial" offering (2:2). Perhaps this means that the offering called to mind the Lord's gracious deeds and enabled the person bringing the offering to confess the name of the Lord in gratitude.

Leviticus 2 contains various recipes for offerings. We should take note of the fact that leaven and honey—which cause decay and therefore symbolize sin and impurity—may *not* be used. But salt, which retards spoiling, could be used (2:11-13). This gives us some idea why Christ said to His disciples: "You are the salt of the earth." (Matt. 5:13; Mark 9:49-50).

Provision is made for simpler food as well as more elaborate food. The person bringing the meal offering was giving the substance of his life, his "daily bread," to the Lord. Because it was given to the Lord, what was left of the offering was not to be eaten by the person who brought the offering. Only the priests, as representatives of Yahweh, were allowed to eat it.

Peace offerings. A third kind of freewill offering was the peace offering made out of gratitude (ch. 3). The ritual of this offering begins in the same way as the burnt offering: the hands laid on the head, the slaughter, and the sprinkling of the blood by the priests (3:1-2). The fat and the kidneys are then given to the Lord as a burnt offering.

The kidneys symbolize the inner thoughts of man. It is clear that this symbol plays an important role in the offering. We should also note that the fat and kidneys are to be laid on "the burnt offering, which is upon the wood of the fire." This is no doubt a reference to the burnt offering made early each morning.

This makes it apparent that the burnt offering is the foundation of the meal that later became part of the "peace offering." Peace or shalom, that is, communion with the Lord, rests on the perfect sacrifice of Christ.

We would do well to read 7:28-38 as we consider the peace offering. The breast and the right thigh of the sacrificed animal were to be given to the Lord in a special way. The priest was to "wave" these parts of the animal in the presence of the Lord. As a representative of the Lord, he would then be allowed to keep them for himself.

What about the rest of the sacrificial animal? The remains of this "peace offering" were eaten by the person bringing the offering. This might seem strange to us, but to the Israelite it was the most natural thing in the world. Hence it is not even mentioned explicitly in the passage we are considering (see 19:6; Deut. 14:23; I Sam. 1:4). First-born animals sacrificed as peace offerings were eaten in or near the court of the tabernacle. Yahweh was the invisible Host who offered His people the hospitality of His table on the basis of the atoning sacrifice.

Sin and guilt offerings. The second major type of sacrifice was the sin offering or guilt offering (4:1—6:7; 6:24-30; 7:1-10). Because sin offerings had a great deal in common with guilt offerings, we can examine these two types of offerings at the same time.

The sin offering emphasized the presence of sin, which is a destructive power in human life, and the necessity of atonement. Such an offering was to be brought after an *unintentional* transgression. (Such a transgression might well be punishable by death.) It was also to be brought after incurring uncleanness caused by birth or death, e.g. after a woman bore a child (12:6, 8) or someone was cured of leprosy (14:10ff).

The ritual used for the sin offering is much the same as that used for the peace offering and the burnt offering. But there are definite differences, especially when it comes to the sprinkling of the blood. The blood had to be sprinkled seven times in the Holy Place, before the *veil* or curtain separating the Holy Place from the Holy of Holies. Blood was also spread on the horns of the *altar of incense.* (Horns are symbols of power.) The rest of the blood was poured at the foot of the *altar of burnt offering.* In this way the blood was brought before the Lord.

On the great Day of Atonement (ch. 16), we see the atoning blood laden with the power of life being put to a further use: it is sprinkled on the ark, which is the Lord's throne in the tabernacle.

What about the sacrificial animal itself? It was a symbolic bearer of sin. While the fat and kidneys were burned on the altar of burnt offering, the rest of the animal would be brought to a clean place outside the camp and burned there. That would do away with the sin. Because of the hand laid on the head, the animal to be sacrificed and the person bringing the sacrifice were one. This was how a sin offering for a priest or for the people would be made (4:1-21). The animal sacrificed would be a young bull.

When sacrifices of lesser importance were brought, the blood was smeared on the horns of the altar of burnt offering, and the flesh could be eaten by priests. Leviticus makes separate mention of a sin offering for rulers (4:22-6) and for the common man (vs. 27ff). The sacrificial animal would normally be a goat or sheep. A poor man, however, would be allowed to offer doves.

The *guilt offering* was brought by someone who was guilty in God's sight in that he had unintentionally taken something that belonged to the Lord or to someone else. The animal sacrificed would be a ram. The guilty party would also have to give back what he had wrongly taken, adding a fifth to it (5:16).

Atonement and forgiveness. In 6:8—7:38 we read various regulations binding for priests involved in sacrifices and offerings. Now that you know something about the various types of offerings, you will realize that

FREEWILL OFFERINGS

TYPE OF OFFERING	PROCEDURE*	MEANING/SIGNIFICANCE
Burnt	Worshiper's hand laid on head. Blood sprinkled on altar in court. Whole animal burned.	A token of dedication, consecration to the Lord.
Meal (cereal)	Part burned. Remainder eaten by priest.	Expression of homage and thankfulness.
Peace	Worshiper's hand laid on head. Blood sprinkled. Fat and kidneys burned. Breast and right thigh given to priests. Remainder eaten by worshiper.	Expression of gratitude and a desire for the maintenance of right relations between God, man and one's neighbor.
Sin	Worshiper's hand laid on head. Priest sprinkled blood against altar in Holy Place and in court. Fat and kidneys burned; the remainder sometimes burned outside camp. Parts occasionally eaten by priests and worshipers.	Obtaining forgiveness for unintentional transgressions.
Guilt (tresspass)		Obtaining forgiveness for social offenses or human injury.

*Cattle, sheep, goats, doves, or pigeons could be used for the blood sacrifices.

Leviticus is not as "dry" as it first appeared to be. How faithfully the Lord provided for His people and priests in prescribing laws for offerings! Israel was thoroughly instructed in the necessity of atonement for sin and the possibilities of a joyful life in virtue of the forgiveness of sins.

Here again we see Christ being preached. Christ is our guilt offering! As a burnt offering, He consecrated Himself completely to God. He is the one who makes it possible for us to have communion with God, as the peace offering's meal in the court of the tabernacle reminds us.

If perfection had been attainable through the Levitical priesthood . . . (Heb. 7:11).

3. The Consecration of the Priests

The high priest's garments. After the offerings came the consecration of the liturgical mediators of the old covenant. Although this subject was already dealt with in Exodus 29, Leviticus 9 goes into it further. The consecration took a week. On each day of that week, various offerings were brought. You will recognize the kinds of offerings immediately.

The ceremony began with the clothing of Aaron and his four sons. As high priest, Aaron wore an undergarment of white linen and a blue outer garment woven as one piece of cloth. Over the upper part of his body he also wore an ephod, a breastplate covered on the front side with twelve precious stones, one for each of the tribes of Israel. The breastplate or satchel held the Urim and Thummim, two precious stones used to determine the Lord's will. On his head the high priest wore a miter or turban, with the words

"Holy to the LORD" engraved on a golden plate fastened to the front (Ex. 28:36). This was a case of clothes "making " the man. The clothes pointed to God's grace in calling the high priest to his most holy office.

After the week of consecration (ch. 8) was over, the day came for the priest to assume his office. This involved a number of offerings: sin offerings, burnt offerings, peace offerings, and cereal offerings. After that the people of Israel were blessed by Aaron. Moses and Aaron then went into the tabernacle. When they came out, they blessed the people again, after which the Lord indicated His acceptance of the sacrificial service: His glory appeared (in accordance with the promise of 9:6) and consumed the offering (9:24).

A liturgical sin. The glory of the Lord also became manifest in another way that day. Nadab and Abihu, the two oldest sons of Aaron, who became priests at the same time as their father, hit upon the idea of adding an extra number to the program of festivities. On their own they decided to bring an *incense offering*.

Were these young men suddenly feeling their own importance? They had been on Mount Horeb after the covenant was made (Ex. 24). Were they perhaps drinking on this great ceremonial day? Some interpreters assume that they were, basing their conclusion on the fact that immediately after this unfortunate episode, Moses declared that priests were to drink no wine or strong drink while "on duty." If they drank, they might lose their powers of discrimination.

In any event, these two young priests added something to the ceremony that day when they assumed office. They brought an "alien," i.e. *unlawful*, fire to the altar. Thereby the priesthood of Aaron's order was imperiled.

At the very beginning, then, it was clear that Aaron's priesthood would be *far from perfect*. There was good reason for establishing sin offerings for priests. If "Aaron" was to continue to serve as priest, it would only be by the grace of the Lord. Aaron had already thrown away the right to be priest.

Total consecration. This serious offense against the order established by Yahweh could not go unpunished. The fire of the Lord killed the two priests in the midst of their transgression. A sin offering would do no good here, for the offense had been committed deliberately. Furthermore, it had to be clear from the outset that no manmade religion or worship would be permitted. Thus we see that the "glory" of the Lord can consume a burnt offering, thereby indicating God's *favor* (9:24), and can also consume priests, thereby indicating God's *wrath* (10:3).

It was a horrible day for Aaron, whereas it should have been a wonderful day. His suffering was made even greater when Moses forbade him to mourn or even attend the burial of his sons. Let the dead bury the dead! The priest is the keeper of the revitalizing anointing oil and therefore must avoid any contact with the uncleanness of death (10:6-7; 21:11-12). Being an office-bearer also means bearing a cross, being totally consecrated to the Lord.

4. Laws to Promote Purity and Holiness

The antithesis. A key concept in Leviticus is "discrimination," that is, the ability to perceive differences. As a member of a holy nation, the Israelite had to learn to distinguish between the clean and the unclean. For us, as members of the modern Western world, this may sound a little strange. Yet, there are factors that make this distinction somewhat understandable.

First of all, the Lord was taking the actual situation into account. (In Noah's time, people already thought in terms of clean and unclean animals.) Second, Israel still had to be *brought up* and *trained*. The Lord wanted to impress it upon Israel that He is holy and therefore hates all sin and death. Third, given the poor hygenic conditions prevailing at that time, many of the regulations can be explained on health grounds (e.g. purification, cleansing, destroying the homes of lepers). Fourth, the background to some of the rules is the *antithesis* between Israel and the *heathen* nations. (The pig, for example, played a role in the worship services of the Babylonians, the Syrians, and the Egyptians.)

"Ceremonial" laws. Much later the Lord made it clear to Peter that the wall between the clean and the unclean was not needed under the new covenant (see Acts 10:9ff; 11:5ff). Today we are no longer bound by all those regulations in Leviticus. The Church is not in its period of infancy anymore; it has grown up. Just as the Church is no longer limited to the people of Israel, it is no longer limited by all those "ceremonial" laws about impurity. Christ fulfilled them once and for all.

But this is not to say that the laws we find in Leviticus have no value for our time. On the contrary, they are part of God's revelation and call for our attention. We see how the Lord brought up His people and instilled in them the notion that they are a holy people (see Ex. 19:6).

The Church of the New Testament is also sanctified and purified by blood (the blood of Christ) although this comes to expression in a different way. All the priestly terms (e.g. *cleansing, purification*) can be applied to the Church of our Lord Jesus. Baptism, which is a washing with water, continues a theme found in Leviticus. "Since we have a great priest over the house of God, let us draw near with a true heart in full assurance of faith, with our hearts sprinkled clean from an evil conscience and our bodies washed with pure water" (Heb. 10:21-2).

Clean and unclean. In Leviticus 11 we find regulations about clean animals and unclean animals. To get a clear idea just which animals are meant, use a fairly recent translation; our knowledge of the Hebrew names for animals has been advanced tremendously since the time when the King James translation was made. We note that the animals that crawl along the earth are generally classed as unclean. Fish that look like snakes are also called unclean.

A guilt offering was to be brought after childbirth (ch. 12). Mary brought such an offering after the birth of Jesus (see Luke 2:24). She used the usual offering of the poor—pigeons. Apparently the wise men from the east had not yet arrived. This regulation was intended to drive home the point that without God's intervention, the clean cannot be born of the unclean. Man is already unclean at birth.

Holiness regulations. Leviticus 13 and 14 deal with leprosy, a horrible disease that could well be characterized as a living death. As a holy people, the Israelites had to live by certain regulations and measures. Offerings were necessary whenever a leper was cured and purified. That's why Christ later sent the lepers He had healed to the priest. It was the priest's duty to check and see whether the leper had in fact been healed. He was also the one through whom the purification offering was made.

If we keep Leviticus 15 in mind as background, the story about the woman who had bled for twelve years makes sense (Matt. 9:20-2). Because of her ailment, this woman was actually excluded from the cultic community. Christ restored her to her full position in life. And this in turn gives us the *key* to Leviticus 15, which is a difficult chapter. The law accentuates the destructive power of sin, which also has its effect on human sexuality. But Christ delivers us from this power, too, and renews us as sexual creatures.

5. Redemption by Blood Alone

The great Day of Atonement. That Christ delivers us, redeems us, and purifies us is clearly reflected by the great Day of Atonement (already mentioned earlier). On this special day there was an extra guilt offering. Because the Letter to the Hebrews alludes repeatedly to the ritual of the great Day of Atonement, we must know something about it.

Once per year the high priest was to enter the Holy of Holies for purposes of atonement. He acted on behalf of himself and his house, but also on behalf of the "congregation of Israel." For himself and his family he would bring a young bull as a guilt offering, just as he had done when he was consecrated to the priesthood, and a ram as a burnt offering.

This time, however, he would not wear all his garments and ornaments. He would wear only his linen undergarment, since it was a day of *penitence.* For the people he would bring two goats as a guilt offering and a ram as a burnt offering.

The Holy of Holies. First the offering for the priest and his household was made. The high priest took the blood of the bull, entered the tabernacle, took fire from the altar of incense, and used it to create a pleasing odor by burning some incense he brought with him. Surrounded by a cloud of incense, he then entered the Holy of Holies and sprinkled part of the blood on the front of the mercy seat above the ark. He also sprinkled blood before the ark seven times. (Seven is a holy number.) He did the same thing with the blood of the goat offered on behalf of the people. The blood of the bull and the goat was then spread on the horns of the altar of burnt offering and sprinkled on the ground seven times again.

The sprinkling of blood on the ground was not superfluous, for on the great Day of Atonement the people were not the only ones purified. Through the blood, the sanctuary itself was also purified of all unholiness (16:20).

The scapegoat. What happened to the other goat? Aaron had to put both his hands on its head, "and confess over him all the iniquities of the people of Israel, and all their transgressions, all their sins; and he shall put them upon the *head of the goat*" (16:21). Thus burdened by the iniquities of Israel, this goat (called the scapegoat) was brought out to the wilderness—and set free! That ended the ceremony of atonement.

After the high priest washed, he brought the burnt offering dressed in his full splendor. The heat of God's anger had been cooled. In a *single day,* the iniquity of the land was removed (Zech. 3:9). Aaron had been granted the privilege of penetrating to God's throne and the domain of the holy angels in order to bring about atonement (see Zech. 3:7).

Aaron	Christ
Offers surrogate blood.	Pours out His own blood.
Performs the sacrificial ceremony repeatedly.	Sacrifices Himself once and for all.
Enters a copy of the heavenly temple.	Ascends to the holiness of heaven itself.
Offers sacrifices out of tradition and in virtue of hereditary succession.	Sacrifices Himself out of pure obedience, called by the Father.

Christ's redemptive work. The Letter to the Hebrews points out that Christ's work represents the last great Day of Atonement. Consider the contrasts on the preceeding page.

Think of the Roman Catholic mass as you consider all of this. The Catholics proceed just as though the definitive offering had never been made. Every day is a "great Day of Atonement," even though the sacrifice brought does not involve blood. They fail to realize that *the* sacrifice has already been made—at Golgotha. The blood has already been sprinkled—offered to the Father.

Do you know when? When Christ ascended to heaven. That's when the last great Day of Atonement came to an end. As Priest and Lamb, Christ approached the throne of God—its parallel on earth is the ark—and was then allowed to *seat* Himself on the throne (see Jer. 30:21, Ps. 110:1).

Kosher. Perhaps you have seen the word *kosher* on the wall of a Jewish butcher shop or hotel. This word means that the institution in question offers meat from animals slaughtered in the prescribed ritual manner.

Because the temple has been destroyed, the Jews can no longer continue their services of sacrifice. Yet the orthodox Jew still maintains the torah wherever it can be applied in daily life. Now, it happens that the torah includes regulations about how animals are to be slaughtered for meat. Because the blood was regarded as the bearer of life (the "soul"), and because it played such a great role in the ceremony of *atonement*, no one was to consume it (17:10ff).

During the years in the wilderness, the blood had to be poured out at the altar. *Every* killing of an animal was actually to be regarded as the bringing of a peace offering (17:5). The blood of an animal killed on a hunt had to be poured out in the field (17:13). Naturally, heathen customs like presenting offerings to the gods of the field were also condemned (17:7).

Through these decrees, the Lord preserved Israel's distinctness and uniqueness during the years in the wilderness. Deuteronomy 12, which also has to do with slaughtering animals, bears more on the conditions in Canaan. Someone who lived too far from the temple was allowed to pour the blood on the ground.

Jews who slaughter animals under the supervision of rabbis continue these practices to this day. But they read the law in a mistaken way, blind to the most important factor of all. The Lamb, Jesus Christ, has been slain in true "kosher" fashion and has fulfilled Leviticus 17! The Lamb bears the sign of a slit throat (see Rev. 5:6).

6. Holiness Required in Daily Life

Life as a unity. In a certain sense, our Western way of thinking violates the unity of creation by placing things in "pigeonholes." We do not see life as a *totality*, for we try to put everything in some compartment or other.

That's not how the Bible looks at reality. In the Bible, life is seen as a unity. That's why the law of holiness as we find it in Leviticus includes regulations about sexual life (ch. 18) as well as peace offerings (19:5-8) and the care of the poor and strangers (19:10).

We also find another concrete elaboration of the decalogue—something that we tend to overlook. Just as in Exodus 20, God begins with the words: "I am the LORD your God." Those same powerful words crop up repeatedly. (Perhaps you should underline them in your own Bible.)

Law and redemption. The commandments are grounded in the Lord's redemptive acts. We must be careful never to lose sight of this point, for many of the commandments were specifically directed against practices current among the Canaanites. The fertility rites of Baal and Astarte sometimes involved temple prostitution and consequently led to disorder and upheaval in all of life. "And you shall not *profane* my *holy* name, but I will be *hallowed* among the people of Israel; I am the LORD who *sanctify* you, who brought you out of the land of Egypt to be your God: I am the LORD" (22:32-3).

Because the Canaanite religions seemed so attractive to the Israelites, we also find an express commandment forbidding the Israelites to worship the god Molech (whose name means *king*) by sacrificing first-born children to him (18:21 and 20:1ff). Wasn't Yahweh the King who made a path for Israel through the sea (Ex. 15:18) and spared the first-born that night when the fearsome plague struck Egypt?

Special laws for priests. Because the worship ceremonies were intended to train Israel to be a *holy* nation, the priests were subject to special laws of holiness. They were to have no physical flaws or blemishes, they were limited in their choice of a wife, and they were not to touch a dead person (ch. 21-22).

The animals used for sacrifices were also to bear the mark of holiness: animals with blemishes were not acceptable for sacrifices (22:17-25; see also Mal. 1:6-14). The Lord would not be content with goods that no one else wanted.* How could an imperfect sacrifice—or an imper-

*The idea of offering an imperfect animal in order to fulfill the obligation with as little expense as possible must also be condemned as following the world's example. The pagans used to do this to deceive their gods and goddesses!

fect priest—be a foreshadowing of our *perfect* High Priest?

Echoes of the law. Before we finish with the "law of holiness," I must remind you that the prophets repeatedly point back to it. For example, the declaration about weights and measures (19:35) finds an echo in Ezekiel 45:10 and Proverbs 11:1. It also forms the basis for the complaints of Amos (Amos 8:5) and Micah (Mic. 6:10). And didn't our highest Priest and Teacher point back to the "law of holiness" when He commanded us to love our neighbors?

When you consider the following incident, you will quickly see how timely and appropriate this law of Moses was. This story about a temple in southern Italy devoted to the goddess Hera is worth more than a laugh. It should make us think: "I sit on a piece of wall and watch the excavators, who examine every fragment as carefully as if it were a piece of gold. What are the treasures unearthed in their midday diggings? A few fragments of a pot, a piece of rusty iron, a bone. To the layman, this refuse of centuries gone by means nothing, but to the archeologist these small items are pages in an exciting book that he must try to decipher. Signora Zancani laughs as she tells me the story of a man who visited this excavation site. This man knew all about the bones of animals—but next to nothing about human bones. His name was Nobis, and he was a scholar from Kiel (Germany). He bent over the bones that had been gathered on the ground near the excavation site, bones from animals that had been offered to the goddess at the place of sacrifice. Herr Nobis found one bone he simply could not identify, and thus he supposed that it must be a human bone. To make sure, he asked if he could take it along to Kiel, in order to look at it further in his laboratory.

"A month later Signora Zancani received a letter from Herr Nobis. The bone had come from a sheep that had broken its leg. The farmer had set the broken leg, but it failed to heal properly. Hence the puzzling shape of the bone.

"Signora Zancani laughed out loud. All at once she saw clearly what sort of thing had been going on 25 centuries ago as the pilgrims came to worship Hera. In order to get off cheaply, some farmer had offered the goddess a crippled sheep. 'The crippled sheep,' laughed Signora Zancani. 'Right down to the deformed bone, it sounds like some lost comedy of Plautus'" (Bertus Aafjes, "Dagboek van Paestum," published in *Elseviers Weekblad*, Dec. 8, 1962).

We must not make the mistake of supposing that Christ was giving a new commandment when He spoke of loving your neighbor as yourself (Matt. 22:37). We already find this commandment in Leviticus 19:18! The Torah even made the bold demand: "You shall not hate your brother in your heart"! (19:17).

Gandhi fell asleep when he reached Leviticus and found nothing else exciting in the Bible until he got to the Sermon on the Mount (Matt. 5-7). If only he had stayed awake, he would already have found the nucleus of the Sermon on the Mount in the third book of Moses.

Behold, on the mountains the feet of him who brings good tidings, who proclaims peace! Keep your feasts, O Judah, fulfill your vows (Nahum 1:15).

7. Israel's Feasts

Feast days. Some of Israel's feasts were already mentioned earlier. Leviticus 23 goes into this matter of the feasts once more on the basis of the main theme of the book, i.e. holiness (see also Ex. 23:14-17; 34:18-24; Num. 28:16—29:39; Deut. 16:1-17). The following feast days are mentioned.

(1) The *sabbath*, which was the seventh day of the week.
(2) The *Passover*, the feast of unleavened bread. The first sheaves were then brought in.
(3) Seven weeks later, on the fiftieth day, came the *Feast of Weeks*, also called the Feast of "Pen-

tecost" because it was celebrated on the fiftieth day (Greek: *pentecosté*).

(4) The *Feast of Trumpets* was held on the first day of the seventh month (approximately October). This seventh month also included the great Day of Atonement, as well as the Feast of Tabernacles. The sound of the trumpet can be a signal of judgment, for it reminds us of the holiness of the Lord. Later this day became the first day of the new year.

(5) The *great Day of Atonement* (23:26-32), which was a day for people to humble themselves.

(6) The *Feast of Tabernacles* (23:33-43) reminded the Israelites of their great journey through the wilderness, a time when they had to live in tents. This feast lasted seven days. It coincided with the end of the fruit and wine harvest and was marked by great gaiety and joy. On the basis of atonement—the Day of Atonement had come and gone—life could flourish. Thus the Feast of Tabernacles was the greatest of all the Jewish feasts. The multitude of people that could not be numbered, all carrying palm branches in their hands (Rev. 7), were like the crowd at the Feast of Tabernacles.

The year of Jubilee. This cycle of feasts did not only involve days but also *years*. Every seventh year was a *sabbath year*. The land would rest, and there would be no pruning or harvesting. And just as the Feast of Pentecost was seven weeks removed from the Passover, there was a year of Jubilee following every seventh sabbath year. Thus this special year came once in 50 years. The year of Jubilee was the year of the ram's horn and would begin with the blowing of this horn.

FEASTS, FESTIVALS AND SPECIAL YEARS*

	Event	Scripture References	When	What/How	Why
Frequent Celebrations	***Sabbath***	Gen. 2:2-3 Ex. 20:8-10 31:12-17 Num. 28:9-10 Deut. 5:12-15	On the 7th day of each week	All work stopped Daily sacrifices doubled	A day of rest consecrated to Yahweh, in commemoration of the completion of creation, and the deliverance from Egypt
Frequent Celebrations	***New Moon Festival*** **and** ***Feast of Trumpets*** **also called** **Day of Acclamation**	Num. 28:11-15 Lev. 23:23-25 Num. 29:1-6	On the 1st day of each lunar month Only on the new moon of the 7th month, Tishri (Sept.-Oct.)	A day of rest with sacrifices, offerings and assemblies In addition to the above, the blowing of trumpets occurred	Consecration and Thanksgiving
The Major Annual Feasts, see Ex. 23:14-16	***Passover*** **and** ***Unleavened Bread***	Ex. 12:1-27, 43-9 Lev. 23:5-8 Num. 9:1-14 28:16-25	Passover: 10th day of first month, Nisan (March-April) Unleavened Bread: the following 7 days (15th-21st)	Sacrifice of a lamb Sprinkling of the blood Unleavened bread from the first barley harvest for one week	Commemoration of Israel's departure from Egypt
The Major Annual Feasts, see Ex. 23:14-16	***Feast of Weeks*** **also called** **Harvest** **First Fruits** **Pentecost**	Lev. 23:9-21	The day after the 7th sabbath from Passover (the 50th day)	First-fruits of the harvest offered to God and leavened bread offered in sacrifice	A joyful celebration of thanksgiving for the completion of the wheat harvest
The Major Annual Feasts, see Ex. 23:14-16	***Feast of Tabernacles*** **also called** **Booths** **Tents** **Huts** **Ingathering**	Lev. 23:33-43	Autumn, after the harvest of fruit and wine; gradually settled down to the 15th-22nd of the 7th month, Tishri (Sept.-Oct.)	The most important and most crowded of the annual feasts; for 7 days they lived in shelters made of branches	Thanksgiving for completed harvests and a reminder of their tent-dwelling days in the wilderness

Later Feasts	***Day of Atonement*** **also called Yom Kippur Day of Expiations**	Lev. 16 23:26-32	10th day of 7th month, Tishri (Sept.-Oct.)	Various rituals for expiation of the people's sins, among them, -the entering of the Holy of Holies by high priest -sending the scapegoat into the wilderness	A time of rededication through confession, penance, fasting, and atonement rituals
	Feast of the Hanukkah **also called Dedication Lights**	Reference in John 10:22	For 8 days beginning Dec. 25	Lamps lit in front of each house—a new one each day till the last day of the feast	After the desecration of the temple in 168 B.C. by Antiochus Epiphanes, this celebration was instituted to mark the purification of the temple
	Feast of Purim	Esther 9	13th-15th of last month, Adar (Feb.-March)	13th: a day of fasting 14th and 15th: general rejoicing and the reading of Esther in the synagogue	Commemoration of the Jews' deliverance from extermination in the Persian Empire
Special Years	***Sabbatical Year***	Lev. 25:1-7	Every 7th year	Land was to rest (lay fallow) Israelite slaves to be freed	To help maintain social and economic justice
	Year of Jubilee	Lev. 25:8-34	At the end of 7 weeks of years (every 50th year)	Land was to rest Property returned to original owners Israelite slaves freed Debts cancelled	

*Information from Roland de Vaux, *Ancient Israel*, Vol. II, pp. 468-517.

The year of Jubilee was an occasion of great joy for any Israelites who had become slaves or had been forced to sell their homes or land because of bankruptcy. They were freed and automatically got their land and property back (ch. 25).

As you can no doubt understand, the year of Jubilee had definite consequences for business. If you bought a piece of land from someone in financial difficulties, you would pay *only* for the estimated value of the number of harvests left until the next year of Jubilee; then the land would have to be returned to its original owner. The price paid would be for the *use* of the land to produce food.

The year of Jubilee was a merciful decree of the Lord. Thus it should not surprise us that the Christ, the servant of the Lord, is depicted in Isaiah as saying, "The LORD has anointed me to bring good tidings to the afflicted . . . to proclaim the year of the LORD's favor" (Is. 61:1-2). The Messiah brings the *year of Jubilee*! From the very beginning of His ministry in Nazareth, Christ used this text to proclaim the gospel. The light of the Messiah burns brightly in Israel's law.

Redemption. That light also breaks through in the regulations about the redemption or buying back of property and slaves. The family had the right—indeed, the *obligation*—to buy back relatives who had become slaves because of their poverty. The family was also to buy back the land and houses of such unfortunates. The Messianic light is clear here: Christ is the great *Redeemer*. He is our brother, our next of kin, and He buys us and delivers us body and soul from satan's power.

The last chapter of Leviticus also deals with the question of buying back. It was possible to take back something once promised or vowed to the Lord—provided, of course, that one paid a certain penalty. We all know what it's like to make a vow. We get into difficulty and promise the

Lord this or that if He will hear our plea for help. Once the crisis has passed, however, we start looking for ways to get out of the promise. The torah was intended to give guidance in this area too. Fulfill your vows to the Lord, O Israel!

8. Covenant Blessing and Covenant Wrath

Judgment or communion. Before the section about vows, we read about *blessings* and *curses* (ch. 26). We find comparable material in Deuteronomy 28 (which was to be read aloud at Shechem, in Canaan).

Israel is free to choose between the way of life and the way of death. Breaking the covenant means calling forth the powers of judgment, e.g. enemies, drought, epidemics, famine. I am Yahweh, your God! But covenant faithfulness means a blossoming of life and communion with the Lord. "And I will walk among you, and will be your God, and you shall be my people. I am the LORD your God, who brought you forth out of the land of Egypt" (26:12-13).

The "law" and the "prophets." What we find in the prophets is nothing but an *elaboration* of this theme. The prophets give us a beautiful perspective on God's redemptive activities and speak of Messianic sabbath rest, but they also tell of hunger, the swōrd and pestilence. In other words, the prophets develop further the theme of covenant blessing and covenant wrath (see, for example, Is. 1:19-20; Ezek. 5; Amos 4:6-11). Even in Revelation, with its seven seals and seven trumpets and seven bowls, we find an echo of the sevenfold wrath mentioned in Leviticus 26:18-39.

The Bible is more *unified* than we realize. If we only keep our eyes wide open, we see again and again how many connections there are between the "law" and the "prophets." Unless we are acquainted with Leviticus 26, we will never gain a proper understanding of the prophecies of the Old Testament prophets, of Christ (e.g. Matt. 24), and of the apostles (e.g. II Thess. 2 and the book of Revelation).

Numbers

1. Israel's Murmurings and God's Gospel

Hebrew numbers. The names of four of the books of Moses are derived from Greek words, some of them in Latinized form. Numbers, however, takes its name from an ordinary English word. (In the Septuagint version of the Old Testament, it is called *Arithmoi,* which means *numbers.*) This name is not an accurate reflection of the contents of the entire book, although it cannot be denied that the book does present us with many numbers.

The meaning of Hebrew numbers is not always as straightforward as one might expect. Scholars have had to devote much attention to this matter. The number 1000, for example, does not always mean a numerical thousand. In its Hebrew form (*eleph*), it can also mean a clan or a large family unit. Just how many people such an *eleph* might include is sometimes hard to determine, but it was usually less than a thousand.

In the wilderness. The Jews sometimes referred to the book of Numbers by means of the fourth word in the book, *Ba-midbar*, which means *in the wilderness*. This is actually a much better name than *Numbers*, for the book deals with the journey through the wilderness.

Yet we should not look for an exact, detailed chronicle. All the Lord wanted to include in the record is what is important from the standpoint of *redemptive history*. This also applies to the other historical sections of the Bible, of course. The Bible was written not to satisfy our curiosity about events long ago but to proclaim the gospel.

Just what is the gospel in Numbers? Isn't Numbers full of judgments on Israel's sins? It certainly is. One of the key words in the book is *murmur*. Numbers could well be called "The Book of Murmurings in the Wilderness." But in and through all the complaining, we see God's patience. He continued to lead His flock like a shepherd. He told them to break camp at Sinai. He led them through the wilderness, training them for the struggle they would face later. The generation that entered the wilderness perished along the way. They did not live to find "rest" in Canaan.

But the nation as such did not perish! More than once the Lord listened to Moses' plea that the people be preserved. Thus it was a new generation that stood at the gateway to the land of promise.

Isn't this a concrete example of the mighty gospel of God's goodness? He does not deal with us after our sins or requite us according to our iniquities.

Let the Lord . . . go in the midst of us (Ex. 34:9).

2. The Lord's Presence among His People

An army on the march. In the church, numerical strength doesn't count for much. David committed a great sin by holding a census to see how large his kingdom had become. This is not to say, however, that any census is wrong as such. The book of Numbers begins with a numbering of the people commanded by the Lord.

Perhaps this census had something to do with taxation (Ex. 30:11-16). It certainly was related to the organization of the army, the order of marching, and the order of encampment around the tabernacle.

When the Israelites were on the move through the wilderness, the *ark* led the way; when they pitched their tents, the *tabernacle* was at the very center. The Levites pitched their tents immediately around the sanctuary, and the other tribes around them. Judah camped on the east side and *led the way* when it came time to break camp and move on. (The Messiah would be born of Judah's line.) The arrangement of the tribes when they were camped could be pictured as follows:

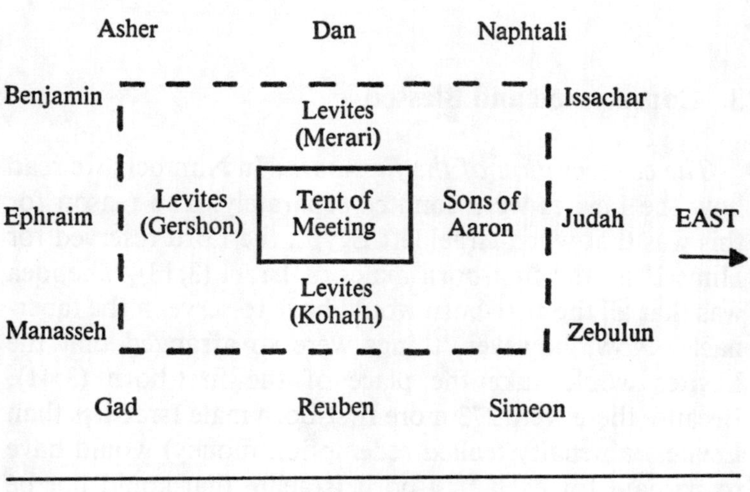

Marching Order

→

Camp of Dan	Camp of Ephraim	Levites with Tent of Meeting	Camp of Reuben	Camp of Judah

God with us. In the arrangement of the camp we see the gospel of Immanuel. We hear an echo of the promise "I will dwell in the midst of you," and are reminded of what we read at the end of the Bible: "Behold, the *tabernacle* of God *is with men*" (Rev. 21:3 KJV). The throne of God and the Lamb will be in the New Jerusalem (Rev. 22:3).

In the book of Numbers, the Levites and priests are still given a place of honor. The priests are to serve in the sacred tent, and the Levites not descended from Aaron are to transport the sacred objects (Num. 1:50-1). In the book of Revelation, however, the differences between the various tribes have fallen away. In their place we find a universal priesthood. "They shall be priests of God and of Christ" (Rev. 20:6). "His [temple] servants shall worship him" (Rev. 22:3).

3. Consecrated and Blessed

The consecration of the first-born. In Numbers we read how the Levites were counted separately. The reason for this was that when Israel left Egypt, the Lord reserved for Himself all the first-born males of Israel (3:13). The idea was that all the first-born would have to serve in the tabernacle. Now, however, things were so arranged that the Levites would take the place of the first-born (3:41). Because there were 273 more first-born male Israelites than Levites, a penalty (called redemption money) would have to be paid for each first-born Israelite that could not be replaced by a Levite. The amount was five shekels (3:46ff).

The payment of this redemption money remained a custom in Israel. In the New Testament we read of Joseph paying the same penalty to free Jesus of this obligation.

Here the priest after the order of Melchizedek was freed from service in Aaron's priestly order: the Redeemer was redeemed! (This is related in Luke 2:23; the sacrifice mentioned in verse 24 was a purification offering on Mary's behalf.)

The Nazirites. In Numbers 5 and 6, we find various regulations connected with the holiness of Israel. In the light of what we have already discussed, these regulations do not need a great deal of explanation. Two aspects, however, require our attention.

First, there is the position of the Nazirites. The Nazirites were to abstain from strong drink. They were not to cut their hair, and (like the high priest) they were not to defile themselves by going near a dead body.

When we hear mention of Nazirites, we usually think of *lifelong* Nazirites, such as Samuel and Samson. Yet the law also provided for the possibility of a man's devoting himself to God for a limited period of his life (see 6:13). After his period as a Nazirite was over, offerings would have to be brought. We read in Acts that Paul also brought such an offering (Acts 21:23ff), which cost him his freedom. (In Acts 18:18 we also find mention of a Nazirite vow.)

A priestly benediction. In Numbers 6:22-7 we are told about the priestly benediction. It is familiar to many of us because it is widely used in churches:

> The LORD bless you and keep you: [singular]
> The LORD make his face to shine upon you, and be gracious to you:
> The LORD lift up his countenance upon you, and give you peace.

In the case of the Nazirites, we are dealing with a consecrated gift that *man* presents to God, but in this benediction, we see God's gift to man. Blessing is the reverse side of curse.

Of course this blessing is not to be thought of as something magic. The Lord blesses us through the Word. But the life and energy He imparts are contingent on obedience to His Word. The Lord will not "keep" us (a term that reminds us of a night watchman and of "the LORD my keeper" in Psalm 121 and of the shepherds "keeping watch" over their flocks by night) if we play games with His Word. If we worship other gods before His face, we need not expect Him to smile down upon us graciously. Instead He will hide His face from us and turn His back on us (see Jer. 18:17). Through the mouth of Isaiah, the Lord castigates His apostate people: "When you spread forth your hands [in prayer], I will hide my eyes from you" (Is. 1:15). We would be better off dead than causing the Lord to hide His countenance from us (Job 13:24; Ps. 27:9; 69:17; Is. 64:7). If we do not look to God as the source of peace and complete happiness, we will never be at peace. The godless have no peace (Is. 48:22; 57:21).

Some scholars have pointed to the harmonic structure of this benediction of the high priest. In the original Hebrew, the three sentences consist respectively of 2 + 1 (= 3), 3 + 2 (= 5), and 4 + 3 (= 7) words, and 3 × 5 and 4× 5 and 5 × 5 letters. This is not a matter of chance. The blessing is amplified and increased as it goes on. The hearer is informed in no uncertain terms that the arm of the Lord is long and His grace unlimited.

The Lord is an overflowing fountain of all good things. Is it any wonder that the psalms repeatedly allude to this benediction of the high priest? (see Ps. 4:6; 31:16; 43:3; 44:3; 67:1; 80:1, 3, 7, 19; 89:15; 118:26; 119:135; see also Rev. 22:4-5). We must await the Lord's blessing. That's what really counts.

Arise, O LORD, and go to thy resting place (Ps. 132:8).

4. The Journey through the Wilderness

The great trek. After the Levites were consecrated and purified (8:5ff) and the Passover was celebrated for the second time (9:1ff), the hour of Israel's departure from Sinai arrived. Trumpets gave the signal (10:1ff). In a cloud that became a pillar of fire by night, the Lord went with His people (9:15-23).

Not Israel but the Lord Himself always gave the signal when it was time to continue the great trek (9:22-3). The ark of the covenant was at the head of the procession. The words Moses always spoke when the procession began are recorded for us: "Arise, O LORD, and let thy enemies be scattered; and let them that hate thee flee before thee" (10:35).

These words are included in a well-known psalm (Ps. 68:1; see also 132:8), which was probably written when the ark was to be transported to Jerusalem. Israel's God was a mighty God of war, taking His place at the head of His people. It's no wonder that John Knox's Scottish Confession of 1560 concludes with these stirring words of Moses: "Arise, O Lord, and let Thine enemies be confounded; let them flee from Thy presence that hate Thy Godly name. Give Thy servants strength to speak Thy Word in boldness, and let all nations attend to Thy true knowledge. So be it."

When the ark came to rest again, Moses declared: "Return, O LORD, to the ten thousand thousands of Israel" (10:36). The New English Bible renders this as follows: "Rest, LORD of the countless thousands of Israel." The meaning of Moses' words is clear: the Lord's presence would *remain* with His people.

Hobab. We also read about a certain Hobab (probably the brother-in-law of Moses) who came along to serve as a guide (10:29-32). Was it human weakness on Moses' part to take along a guide? The Bible certainly does not conceal the flaws in Moses' character. Yet this precaution on the part of Moses may well have been justified.

The Lord likes to work through human and natural means. Even if the cloud always gave the signal to depart or stay put, living in the wilderness did create a number of problems. Streams and pastures would have to be found. Contacts would have to be made with caravans and nomadic tribes. Hobab could be of great service in such matters.

We should not think of the wilderness through which the Israelites passed as a vast expanse of sandy desert. We could better think of it as dry prairie country like a Russian steppe or an African veldt. The territory crossed by the Israelites in their great trek was a land of small bushes and unsightly little trees, but it did have vegetation that sheep could feed on. As for Hobab, his family later became part of Israel: Jael, the woman who killed Sisera (Judges 4:11-23), was one of his descendants.

When your fathers tested me . . . (Ps. 95:9).

5. Years of Wandering and Discontent

Complaining and murmuring. God was incredibly gracious to the Israelites, but they stumbled and fell repeatedly. Numbers 11:1-3 speaks of the general complaining and murmuring.

The Israelites found that the edge of their camp had caught fire. At the request of the people, Moses prayed to the Lord and the fire was extinguished.

Later the murmuring began again. Some of the people who had tagged along when the Israelites departed from Egypt now began to idealize the land they had left behind; they dreamed of fish and watermelons and other food no longer available. Such talk had its effect on the Israelites. The manna provided by God seemed like meager fare in comparison. Soon the Israelites were swept along in this ungrateful nostalgia. They stood crying like children in the doors of their tents. Who will give us meat to eat? We had it so good in Egypt!

Seventy elders. Such talk aroused the wrath of the Lord. At the same time, Moses became fed up with the attitude of the people. He was ready to throw in the towel and step down as leader. He complained that it was not fair of the Lord to give him the responsibility of leading such a people and caring for them.

The Lord answered that He was willing to lighten Moses' task by transferring some of the Spirit resting on him to 70 elders. Moreover, the Lord promised to provide meat; He would let the Israelites eat so much meat that they would come to loathe it. Moses did ask some questions out of unbelief, just as the disciples of Jesus were later to do when He used a few loaves of bread and a couple of fish to feed thousands of people. But the Lord was easily capable of doing what He had promised; His hand was not shortened (11:23).

The elders on whom the Spirit now rested prophesied at the tabernacle. Even two other men seemed to have the Lord's Spirit in them and began to prophesy. An overly zealous Joshua wanted Moses to forbid them, but Moses responded with what amounts to a Pentecost prayer: "Would that all the LORD's people were prophets, that the LORD would put his spirit upon them!"

Graves of lust. What about the meat promised to the Israelites? It came in the form of quails driven to the camp by a strong wind. The quails flew just above the camp and could easily be caught. Some of them even fell to the ground on their own.

This gift again led Israel to *stumble*. The Israelites devoured the birds as greedily as if they had been starving to death on their diet of manna. Therefore the Lord sent them a severe plague. As a result, that place came to be known as *Kibroth-hattaavah*, which means *graves of lust*.

Miriam's jealousy. That was not the end of the difficulties. Miriam and Aaron got into a dispute with Moses because of his marriage to a Cushite woman. Did they have something against this "foreigner"? Or were they defending Zipporah, the Midianite woman Moses had married many years before? Or was the question of a wife perhaps an excuse to stir up some trouble for Moses? Whatever the reason, both Miriam (Moses' older sister) and Aaron (his brother and spokesman) disputed his monopoly as prophet. "Has the LORD not spoken through us also?"

It turned out that the Lord Himself had to intervene in this matter. He summoned the three to the tent of meeting, where He made it clear that Moses was to be the leader. "If there is a prophet among you, I the LORD make myself known to him in a vision, I speak with him in a dream. Not so with my servant Moses; he is entrusted with all my house. With him I speak mouth to mouth, clearly, and not in dark speech; and he beholds the form of the LORD" (12:6-8).

Let there be no complaints about Moses, then! The haughty Miriam was punished: she became a leper. Moses had to step in as mediator and implore God in prayer to heal her.

New Testament and Numbers 12. In the New Testament there are two references to this story. First of all, Hebrews

3:1-6 compares Christ and Moses, each of whom was faithful in the house of God (the church) in his own way. Moses was faithful as a *servant,* but Christ was faithful as the *Son,* keeping the "house" in order and maintaining it.

The other place is I Corinthians 13:12, where we read: "For now we see in a mirror dimly, but then face to face. Now I know in part; then I shall understand fully, even as I have been fully understood." In Corinth there were people who had a high opinion of their abilities as prophets and prophetesses. What Paul was telling them is this: "That's all well and good. Yet those forms are only temporary. We must not make the mistake of thinking that we can know everything. Our existence is fragmentary. Not until Christ's return will we know the Lord as Moses knew Him, that is, without the mediation of mysterious reflections in a dim mirror. We shall see the Lord face to face."

Twelve spies. The story of Israel's murmuring and complaining is not yet at an end. The Israelites were nearing the promised land. Twelve spies were sent out. They returned with a majority report and a minority report. The majority recommended against an invasion because of the military superiority of the Canaanites. The minority (Joshua, of the tribe of Ephraim, and Caleb, of the tribe of Judah) were in favor of an invasion. They based their expectation of success on God's promises.

The majority report led to unrest and rebellion among the Israelites. "Let us choose a captain and go back to Egypt." Such talk aroused the Lord's wrath: He wanted to make a great nation of Moses instead. But Moses begged the Lord not to destroy Israel. He pleaded with God for 40 days (Deut. 9:25), the same period of time he spent receiving the law and repenting after Israel's sin of worshiping the calf (see Deut. 9:9, 18).

Moses used two main arguments in his plea. First, what would the nations say? Wouldn't they say that the Lord is unable to keep His oath and promises? Second, after the sin at Sinai the Lord had spoken of Himself as slow to anger and abounding in steadfast love (see Ex. 34:6-7).

Punishment for unbelief. The Lord listened to the prayer of Moses and forgave the Israelites once more. But at the same time He swore an oath that those who would rather die in the wilderness would get their way (14:2, 28-30). Except for Joshua and Caleb, the entire wilderness generation would perish before the entry into Canaan.

An attempt was then made to invade Canaan anyway, but because it did not have the Lord's blessing, it failed (14:39ff). The spies had been gone on their mission for 40 days. For each of those days, the Israelites would now have to spend a year in the wilderness.

The grace that God showed the Israelites here in sparing them was indeed great. The New Testament reminds us:

> They were unable to enter *because of unbelief.* Therefore, while the promise of entering his rest remains, let us fear lest any of you be judged to have failed to reach it. For good news came to us just as to them; but the message which they heard did not benefit them, because it *did not meet with faith* in the hearers (Heb. 3:19—4:2).

Korah, Dathan and Abiram. It did not meet with faith! Isn't this what we see again and again in the story of the wilderness? Think of the rebellion of Korah, Dathan and Abiram (ch. 16-17).

Korah was a Levite. He was of the opinion that those who were Levites could also be priests. Dathan and Abiram were from the tribe of Reuben. (Reuben was Jacob's first-born son.) They understood the "office of all believers" as meaning that all believers could be priests. All Israelites were "holy." Wasn't that what the Lord had declared earlier? (see Ex. 19:6). Wasn't Israel a kingdom in which everyone was a priest?

Now, Korah did not have the very same goals in mind as Dathan and Abiram, but the three were united in their opposition to Moses and Aaron. (Such unholy alliances have been made throughout history to this very day, which is part of the reason for the revolutions in the political arena and the disorder in the church.)

Another factor at work in this rebellion was dissatisfaction at being sent on such a long journey that seemed to be leading nowhere. Dathan and Abiram even went so far as to speak of *Egypt* as a land of milk and honey. This statement must have been galling to the Lord, for in His promises and in the reports of the spies, *Canaan* was the land of milk and honey!

God Himself had to settle the issue. Korah and his followers brought an incense offering. Aaron did the same (16:16-18). But the fire of the Lord consumed Korah and his followers (vs. 35). The odor of their incense was apparently no protection against the Lord's burning wrath.

The Israelites who had gathered to watch were instructed to stay away from Korah's tents and from the tents of Dathan and Abiram as well. The latter, together with their families and households, were then swallowed up by the earth (16:25-34). From this it was clear that Moses had indeed been called by God. The Lord had indicated clearly that Moses was His servant called to lead the people, and also that Aaron belonged to Him in a special way, that Aaron was holy and was called to serve as priest (vs. 5).

New Testament application. At this point we turn our attention again to the New Testament, where we find references to this story. In a discussion of heretics and their destructive effect on the church, Paul utters some powerful words: "But God's firm foundation stands, bearing this seal: 'The Lord knows those who are his,' and, 'Let every one who names the name of the Lord depart from iniquity'" (II Tim. 2:19). This is clearly an allusion to the rebellion against the leadership of Moses: the Lord faithfully maintains His office-bearers in the church (16:5). He knows who belong to Him.

On the other hand, the church is called to avoid heretics just as much as Israel was called to stay away from Korah, Dathan and Abiram when God's judgment was about to strike them. The Letter of Jude, which also deals with apostasy, mentions the danger of "perishing in Korah's rebellion" (vs. 11).

Aaron's office maintained. After this dramatic judgment, one would not expect to see further opposition to Moses and Aaron. But a rebellious spirit is not easily broken. The next day Moses and Aaron were reproached in "pious" terms for "killing the people of the LORD." Korah, Dathan and Abiram may have been heretics, but they were apparently well liked.

The people gathered by the tabernacle. Again the glory of the Lord appeared. Once more the Lord proposed to destroy the entire nation, but Aaron, as high priest, atoned for the nation's sin by burning incense.

In order to make it abundantly clear that Aaron was to be high priest, Moses was commanded by God to invite the head of each tribe to leave his staff in the tent of the testimony overnight, together with Aaron's staff. When the staffs were examined the next morning, it was found that Aaron's had produced blossoms and bore ripe almonds!

We already came across the almond tree in connection with the lampstand in the Holy Place of the tabernacle. This tree, which blossoms early, is a symbol of the Lord's faithfulness and watchfulness. The staff that blossomed was to be kept in front of the ark as a permanent token of Aaron's calling.

Moses as magician. Later in the book of Numbers we hear more about this staff that was kept in the Lord's presence. For the umpteenth time, there was unrest and discontent in the ranks of the Israelites. The people complained that there was no water. Moses, with Aaron beside him, was to call the people together, take that same rod in his hand, and give the command for water to flow from the rock.

In this situation, Moses made the biggest mistake of his life. Instead of *speaking* to the rock and thereby demonstrating the power of the Word of the Lord, he struck the rock twice with Aaron's rod and asked, "Shall *we* bring forth water for you out of this rock?" By this course of action, Moses (with Aaron) was presenting himself as a wonder-worker who could make water flow from a rock. Moses had assumed the role of magician.

For this transgression he did not escape punishment. The Lord decreed that neither Moses nor Aaron would enter the land of Canaan. Miriam had already died (20:1), and Aaron soon followed her into the grave (20:22-9). His son Eleazer succeeded him as high priest. And before the entry into Canaan, Moses was to die on Mount Nebo.

As Moses lifted up the serpent in the wilderness, so must the Son of man be lifted up (John 3:14).

6. The Gospel Message in Numbers

The bronze serpent. At the border of Canaan, after one victory in battle had already been won (21:1-3), the grumbling began again. The manna which the Lord provided was now called "worthless food" (21:5).

The Lord responded to this complaint by sending fiery serpents. The people finally appealed to Moses for help, and he was allowed to save them by making a bronze serpent and setting it up on a pole where everyone could see it. Anyone who was bitten by a snake but looked at the bronze serpent would survive.

When Jesus talked to Nicodemus about what it means to be born again, He referred to this story. Nicodemus wanted to know how a second birth is possible (John 3:9), and Jesus answered by pointing to the story of the bronze serpent. Just as Moses lifted up the bronze serpent in the wilderness, the Son of man (i.e. the Christ) would have to be lifted up (i.e. on the cross and in His ascension into heaven), so that all who *believe* could have eternal life and be born again. Haven't we all been bitten by satan, that great serpent, and hasn't the elevated and exalted Messiah given us a new existence?

Living by grace. We must *live* by God's grace. This is the message of the "book of murmuring and complaining," as Paul's commentary makes clear:

> I want you to know, brethren, that our fathers were all under the cloud, and all passed through the sea, and all were baptized into Moses in the cloud and in the sea, and all ate the same supernatural [Greek: Spiritual] food and all drank the same supernatural [Spiritual] drink. For they drank from the supernatural [Spiritual] Rock which followed them, and the Rock was Christ. Nevertheless with most of them God was not pleased; for they were overthrown in the wilderness.
>
> Now these things are warnings for us, not to desire evil as they did. We must not put the Lord to the test, as some of them did and were destroyed by serpents; nor grumble, as some of them did and were destroyed by the Destroyer. Now these things happened to them as a warning, but they were written down for our instruction, upon whom the end of the ages has come. Therefore let any one who thinks that he stands take heed lest he fall (I Cor. 10:1-6, 9-12).

The call for a Mediator. The gospel message contained in the book of Numbers cannot remain hidden from us if we read carefully. All the complaints, all the challenges to Moses' office show us how difficult a prophet's work is and what a difficult road the great Prophet Jesus had to travel.

Like Moses, Jesus was mighty in words and deeds; He was the Mediator of the new covenant. But what opposition He met among His own people! The series of events described in the book of Numbers reflects the way of the cross. Isn't that gospel?

We also find gospel in chapter 19, where we read about the purification water made from the ashes of the red heifer. The red heifer—red is the color that symbolizes life—was to be slaughtered outside the camp as a kind of sin offering. The blood would be sprinkled seven times in front of the tent of meeting. The rest of the heifer would be burned, together with some cedarwood, hyssop (probably a sweet marjoram oil) and scarlet stuff, until there was nothing but ash left. The ash was then used to make *purification water*, which would be sprinkled on the third and seventh days over anyone who had defiled himself by touching a dead body.

In the Letter to the Hebrews we find a reference to this purification ceremony:

> For if the sprinkling of defiled persons with the blood of goats and bulls and with the ashes of a heifer sanctifies for the purification of the flesh, how much more shall the blood of Christ, who through the eternal Spirit offered himself without blemish to God, purify your conscience from dead works to serve the living God (Heb. 9:13-14).

Remember, my people, what Balak king of Moab schemed against you, and how Balaam son of Beor answered him (Mic. 6:5 NEB).

7. Israel Blessed through Balaam

Two victories. We also hear gospel in the prophecy of Balaam. The story behind this prophecy is an interesting one. The Israelites could not pass through the land of the Edomites because they were refused permission by this brother nation. Sihon, the king of the Amorites, wouldn't let them pass through his land either. Therefore Israel defeated him in battle and occupied his territory. Later some of the tribes settled in this area.

Og, the king of Bashan, was also defeated (Num. 21). Israel then camped on the flat plains of Moab, at the entryway to Canaan. Take a look at a map of the area, and the situation will quickly become clear to you.

Balak. The Israelites were perceived as a grave threat by Balak, the king of the Moabites. The news that Sihon and Og had been defeated made a deep impression on him. With his own eyes, Balak could see how numerous the Israelites were.

Now, good advice does not come cheap. Whoever is not strong must rely on cunning instead. Thus Balak resolved to try magic instead of force. Together with the elders of the Midianites, a neighboring people, he sent for a certain seer named Balaam, who lived somewhere by the Euphrates River, and asked him to *curse* Israel.

Balaam. Balaam was clearly motivated by the love of money. But the Lord overpowered him in such a way that he could say nothing but what the Lord put in his mouth. The episode of the talking donkey (22:23ff) was intended to make it clear to Balaam that he had no choice but to speak the Word of Yahweh and ignore the wishes of his employer Balak.

After much hocus-pocus (23:1ff), Balaam finally spoke, but the words that came to his lips were words of blessing rather than curses. From the heights, the prophet looked out over the camp of the Israelites. The promises made to Abraham and Jacob had been fulfilled. "Who can *count* the dust of Jacob, or *number* the fourth part of Israel?" (vs. 10).

Of course Balaam's benediction met with Balak's displeasure. He took Balaam from one hilltop to the other in an effort to get him to curse Israel. Balaam finally explained straightforwardly: "Behold, I received a command to bless: he has blessed, and I cannot revoke it" (23:20).

It was clear that God was with the Israelites. Theirs was the excitement of a people led by a king (23:21). Therefore Balak need not expect them to suffer some catastrophic setback.

Balaam went on to compare Israel to a lion. When he spoke for a third time, he used the image of the lion again and said of Israel: "Blessed be every one who blesses you" (24:9).

A star and a scepter. Balak was most displeased and vexed by this turn of events. Then Balaam spoke a fourth time—this time without preliminary offerings. The seer focused on Israel's future and caught a glimpse of a kingly figure:

> I see him, but not now;
>   I behold him, but not nigh:
> a star shall come forth out of Jacob,
>   and a scepter shall rise out of Israel (24:17).

This appears to be a general vision of the Israelite

kingship. The other nations, of course, had kings before Israel (see Gen. 36:31; I Sam. 8:5). When Israel did receive David as king, he conquered Moab and Edom.

But this prophecy did not yet reach its fulfillment in David. It was Christ who fulfilled what Balaam saw. Just think of the wise men who came from the east. In a sense they were colleagues of this visionary priest Balaam. They saw a new *star* and perceived a connection between this phenomenon and the birth of a *King* in Israel: the *star* and the *scepter* belong together. Christ is the bright morning star who rules the nations with a rod of iron (Rev. 22:16; 12:5). The gospel as presented in the book of Numbers fits right in with the gospel as we find it in the book of Revelation.

Then up stood Phinehas to intervene, and the plague was checked (Ps. 106:30 JB).

8. Succumbing to the Sin of the Midianites

The service of Baal-peor. The Israelites went astray again as they were camped in the flat plains of Moab. The nation that had been so richly blessed allowed itself to be misled, falling into idolatry and apostate religion, the two related dangers that were never far away in the Canaanite world.

It is apparent from 31:16 that Balaam finally advised Balak to try to break the power of the Israelites by enticing them into the sensual service of Baal-peor. In the New Testament, the conduct of Balaam is compared to that of those who misled the church into spiritual idolatry and the worship of idols, thereby inviting compromise with the synagogue of satan (Rev. 2:14). Paul, too, refers to this incident by mentioning the punishment to which it led (I Cor. 10:8).

Phinehas. The leaders of the people were punished by hanging, while the people themselves were struck with a plague that the Bible does not describe for us (25:2ff). At this critical point, Phinehas, the grandson of Aaron, intervened by stabbing one of the leaders of the tribe of Simeon to death, together with the Midianite princess he had taken as his wife.

Not only did this decisive deed bring an end to the plague, it also led the Lord to make a beautiful promise to Phinehas. Because of his zeal for the Lord, he was promised that the office of high priest would always be held by someone of his line. The Lord made a "covenant of peace with him" (25:12-13; see also Ps. 106:30-1; Mal. 2:4-7) and lived up to this promise. The priest bringing the offering of atonement was always a descendant of Phinehas—until Christ made this offering unnecessary through His sacrificial death on the cross.

The sin into which the Midianites had led the Israelites prompted the Lord to order a war of extermination against them (25:16ff). Like the Amalekites, these dangerous people would have to be wiped out. In a raid on the Midianites, the seer Balaam was killed (31:8). Thus his wish of dying a righteous death (see 23:10) was not granted.

He gave their land to Israel
(Ps. 136:21 NEB).

9. Preparing for Possession of the Land

Dividing the conquered land. It is not difficult to find gospel in the rest of the book of Numbers either. Measures had to be taken in connection with the land east of the Jordan, which the Israelites had acquired by defeating Sihon and Og in battle. Preparations also had to be made for taking over Canaan itself, which had not yet been conquered.

Joshua was named as Moses' successor. He was "confirmed" as successor by the laying on of hands (27:15ff). Caleb, the other author of the "minority report," was among those who participated in the division of the new land.

The Levites were assigned a number of cities. Some of their cities were to be places of asylum for anyone who had killed a person by accident (ch. 35).

Property rights. If a man had daughters but no sons, his daughters could inherit his property: women were not to be denied their share in the new land (27:1-11). But they were not to marry outside their own tribe (Num. 36). Thus the tribes were to remain separate, each with its own inalienable territory. The Lord guaranteed His people their rights in the land of promise.

In this we see a foreshadowing of the work of the other Joshua, who was also called Christ. (*Jesus* is a later Greek version of the name *Joshua*.) Because Israel in its sin had forfeited its right to the inheritance, He has made a new Israel (in the form of the Church) that will be able to enter the heavenly Canaan, i.e. the new heaven and the new earth. Because of Him, we have an unshakable right to this inheritance.

Deuteronomy

1. The Book of Covenant Renewal

A perspective on the past. The name *Deuteronomy* means *second law* or *repetition of the law.* In chapter 5 the decalogue is recorded once more. Many other familiar laws pass before us again as well.

Yet the book of Deuteronomy is not a word-for-word repetition of the laws already given earlier. Deuteronomy has a character of its own. When we compare it with the earlier books of Moses, we find that it differs from them in much the same way that the Gospel according to John differs from the other three "Gospels."

Such a difference, of course, is not easy to characterize. I could perhaps begin by pointing out that very little "happens" in Deuteronomy. In effect the book is a long, long sermon delivered by Moses. In the Gospel according to John, likewise, we read some of the sermons of Christ.

The words of Moses recorded in Deuteronomy cast a certain light on Israel's history. They give us a better perspective on the past. The same could be said of the Gospel according to John. Deuteronomy and John are also alike in that both speak repeatedly of the love of God.

A sermon. What Deuteronomy gives us then, is a sermon delivered by Moses. The very first verse of the book makes it apparent that Moses delivered this address shortly before his death. The Israelites were camped on the flat plains of Moab. Canaan was on the other side of the Jordan, which had not yet been crossed. Sihon and Og had already been defeated, as we see from the reference to Og's bedstead (3:11), which seems to have become a museum piece. The sin of Baal-peor described in Numbers 25 had already taken place (4:3ff). This episode had made it clear how vulnerable the Israelites were to the seductive religious practices of the Canaanites.

The *nomadic* nation of Israel was soon to become an *agricultural* people. The Israelites would have to change their ways. Would they now be tempted to embrace the gods of the *land*? The worship of these gods was exciting and enchanting; the Israelites longed to join in the feasts of the Canaanites. In the past the Canaanite gods had bestowed rain on the land and made it fruitful. Wouldn't the Israelites have to pay homage to these gods as well in order to be successful as farmers?

At Baal-peor it had become clear that Israel was in definite danger of violating its status as a nation set apart, of casting its uniqueness aside. How would things go in Canaan? Surely not all the people in Canaan would be wiped out immediately. If not, there was a real danger that the Israelites might preserve the service of Yahweh *in name* while sliding into heathen practices *in fact*.

The Bantu example. A look at the Bantu world of our time can illuminate this matter for us. There are a great many sects among the Bantus in southern Africa. It is typical of many of these sects that they mix "Christianity" with the old Bantu religion. A vague appeal to the Bible is a sufficient excuse to justify the old magical purifications and to introduce a complex hierarchy of office-bearers such as used to exist in the ancient tribal structure. It is not to be denied that these people are religious in a significant sense. Yet, despite their contact with Christianity, they have sunk back into the morass of a false religion.

The same could easily have happened to the Israelites. If you read Judges and Kings, for example, it soon becomes apparent that the service of the true God was mixed with false religions in just this way. Israel adapted itself to the Canaanite religion. Wherever there were heathen places of sacrifice, the name *Baal* was eliminated and *Yahweh* put in its place. Once this surface change was accomplished, the old religion continued as before. To make things simple, it was sometimes even declared: Yahweh = Baal.

"Natural religion." We should also think of the practices of certain Roman Catholic missionaries as we consider this danger. A holy statue is placed in the heathen cultic centers, and the original heathen religion is then allowed to continue in a "Christianized" form.

It is not without reason that the Roman Catholics appear to make such progress on the mission field, for the gospel they present seeks to build on the "natural religion." Willingly they make use of any points of contact they can find, on the assumption that the natural man is not as corrupt and depraved as many Protestants seem to think.

An appeal for faithfulness. We must read the book of Deuteronomy against the background of these dangers. It is a continuous appeal to remain faithful to Yahweh. The religion of the pagans is worthless! Have nothing to do with the gods of the land and the Baals of fertility! Maintain the antithesis! Be intolerant and uncompromising in the face of any false religion. Be consistent, and show your firmness in your allegiance to the Lord. Don't live by manmade religions; live by the torah, the Word of the

Lord. Worship Yahweh and keep His covenant. And treat your neighbor, your brother, as he expects you to.

Long ago the Lord had made a covenant with the patriarchs. Later a covenant was made with Israel at Mount Horeb. Now a new generation stood ready to enter Canaan, that heathen land. Therefore the ceremony of entering into a covenant was repeated on the flat plains of Moab.

The words of Moses as recorded in Deuteronomy form the introduction to this covenant. They contain the terms of the covenant or agreement, describing the rights and obligations of the covenant partners and emphasizing the dangers of not living up to the covenant.

Moses delivered this oration at a very critical moment. Israel, as a vassal, renewed the covenant with Yahweh, its God and Great King. The words of Moses were to be used as a criterion to evaluate the events in Israel's later history. Did Israel remain faithful to the words of that covenant?

2. The Lord's Covenant with His People

Treaties and covenants. The Lord can control what goes on in the hearts of kings just as carefully as a sprinkler controls a forced water irrigation system (Prov. 21:1). He guided the course of history in such a way that when He made His covenant with Israel, there was a certain accepted way of drawing up a political treaty or agreement between nations.

Thanks to the excavations made by archeologists, various treaties have been recovered from the time of the later Hittite empire, i.e. 1450-1200 B.C., which is about the time of Israel's exodus from Egypt. Some of the treaties were between kings who were roughly equal in power (e.g. Ramses II of Egypt and the Hittite king Hattusilis III). Such a treaty could be called a *covenant of parity*. But it also happened that the great Hittite king, for example, would make a covenant with subject leaders and nations. In such a covenant or treaty, he would be the *suzerain*, the lord to whom homage was due.

A covenant made with a vassal or "protectorate" would be called a *suzerainty covenant,* for it was not a treaty between two *equal* partners. The vassal was a defeated subject and was allowed to choose between complete extermination and entering into some sort of brotherly relationship with the great king.

Scholars have unearthed also a treaty made by the Assyrian king Ezarhaddon in 672 B.C., in which the king had his vassals swear an oath that they would continue to recognize his dynasty after his own death and would obey the crown prince once he became king. This was a covenant that involved the succession to the throne. The terms of the covenant binding on the vassals were written as commands: "Thou shalt . . . . Thou shalt not . . . .".

Elements of a suzerainty covenant. When the Lord made His covenant with Israel, He drew on the forms then current in diplomatic circles. In this treaty or covenant, He presented Himself as the Great King, the Suzerain, over against Israel, the vassal.

Because it is so important for us to grasp this point if we are to understand God's revelation in the Bible, I will list the elements or parts that were always to be found in a Hittite suzerainty covenant.*

---

*Readers who would like to pursue this matter further should consult Meredith G. Kline, *The Structure of Biblical Authority* (Grand Rapids, 1972); and C. Vonk, *De Voorzeide Leer,* I-A (Barendrecht, 1960), pp. 314ff, I-B (1963), pp. 504ff, and I-C (1966), pp. 307ff and 403ff.

(1) An *introductory section*: the great king presents himself as the sun and as a great hero. The usual stereotyped opening line is: "These are the words of . . . ."
(2) A *historical section*: the great king explains how good he has been to his vassal, how he has conferred power and land upon him. Demarcations of borders are sometimes discussed in this section.
(3) The *terms of the covenant*: absolute faithfulness and loyalty demanded. The great king spells out just what this involves. Some attention is also given to the question of the succession to the throne. There is to be no rebellion against the successor of the great king.
(4) A *list of witnesses*: gods are mentioned as well as heaven and earth.
(5) *Blessings and curses*: if the covenant is broken, certain sanctions are to be put into effect. This also involves an oath on the part of the vassal.
(6) Provision is made for *regular reading aloud* and proper *preservation* of the covenant document. No part of the text is to be changed. The "tables of the covenant" must be safeguarded in a temple. On certain specified occasions, the vassal must come to the court to hear the treaty read aloud and swear his oath anew. The seal of the dynasty is placed on the official documents.

The Great King. When you compare this sketch of the parts of a suzerainty covenant with the Lord's way of dealing with His people, you see immediately that He acts in the style of a great king. The introductory formula (1) corresponds to the words: "I am the LORD your God."

Both Exodus 19:4-6 and the prologue to the ten commandments give us a (redemptive) historical prologue (2).

The Lord identifies Himself as the one who "brought you out of the land of Egypt, out of the house of bondage."

The "law" can then be seen as the stipulations and terms of the covenant (3). There are blessings and curses (5) to be found at the end of the second commandment, as well as in Leviticus 26.

The tables of the covenant were to be deposited in the ark (6). The law was to be read aloud regularly, and the covenant was renewed from time to time (6). The prophets were authorized by the Great King to call the people to obey the terms of the covenant and to threaten them with covenant wrath if they did not.

This style of the Great King, the King of kings, continues all the way through the book of Revelation. At the very end of the Bible we read a stiff warning: "If any one takes away from the words of the book of this prophecy . . . ."

Imperial style. This style of the Great King comes through especially in Deuteronomy. The Great King makes a covenant with Israel as His vassal. At the same time, the covenant designates Joshua as Moses' successor.

Consider the following resemblances between the covenant in Deuteronomy and the Hittite suzerainty covenants.

(1) Introductory formula: "These are the words . . . ."
(2) The redemptive historical prologue (ch. 1-4) deals with the events from Sinai on.
(3) The terms of the covenant are given in chapters 5-26. The Ten Words form the point of departure. Both the first part of this section and the second (which begins with ch. 12) conclude with some words of blessing and curse.
(4) Witnesses are listed in 30:19 and 31:21ff.
(5) Blessing and curse are dealt with in chapters 11, 27, 28, 32, and 33.

(6) Provision for reading the covenant book aloud and keeping it in a safe place is made in 31:9-13, 26. Furthermore, 4:2 and 12:32 also deal with the obligation of taking good care of the covenant in the exact form in which it was originally given. Just as we saw in connection with the first covenant at Sinai (Ex. 24:4) and also the second covenant (Ex. 34:27), the emphasis falls on the importance of keeping a careful record of everything (27:3, 8; 28:58, 61; 29:20ff; 30:10; 31:9, 19, 21, 24). God will not stand for carelessness or human willfulness. There was to be no "new morality" in Israel.

3. Redemptive Historical Prologue and Constitution

Historical review. Within the framework of covenant renewal, Moses reviews the events that occurred after Israel entered into the covenant at Sinai. In the opening chapters of Deuteronomy, which come before the reiteration of the Ten Words, he shows how graciously the Lord dealt with His stubborn people. Thus the phrase "By grace alone" can also be used to characterize what we read in Deuteronomy.

This grace should lead Israel to hold on to the "peace" and "rest" which the Lord gives to those who keep His torah. "For what great nation is there that has a god so near to it as the LORD our God is to us, whenever we call upon him? And what great nation is there, that has statutes and ordinances so righteous as all this law [or better: teaching, torah] which I set before you this day?" (4:7-8).

Deuteronomy 4 further reminds the Israelites how the Lord revealed Himself at Sinai. He could not be *seen*; only

His voice could be heard (4:15, 12). Therefore the Israelites were not to worship any idols or images of false gods, nor were they to make images of Yahweh. His service is a *service of the Word.* "Did any people ever hear the voice of a god speaking out of the midst of the fire, as you have heard, and still live?" (4:33).

The constitution. When did the people hear the voice of the Lord? When the Ten Words were spoken. These ten commandments form the constitution of the covenant, as it were. Therefore we can well understand why Moses would want to go over them once more (5:6-21).

When we read in 5:3 that the Lord made a covenant not with "our fathers" but with "us, who are all of us here alive this day," we must not take this to mean that no covenant was made with the patriarchs. No, the point Moses wanted to emphasize was that the covenant made at Sinai is just as relevant to *later generations* as to those who were actually present at Sinai. No child could say that the Ten Words and the covenant made at Sinai had nothing to do with him.

In Exodus 20 the fourth commandment is based on God's rest after the six days of creation, but in Deuteronomy 5 we find an argument borrowed from the re-creation, the deliverance from bondage in Egypt. The Israelites were freed from slavery in Egypt, and therefore, out of gratitude, they must allow their own servants a day of sabbath rest. Here we see an example of the social emphasis in the book of Deuteronomy. We will come across more examples later.

4. Israel's Covenant Partner

One Lord. Perhaps you have heard of the Jewish prayer called the "Shema." According to Jewish tradition, every adult male is to say this prayer each morning and evening. The prayer is composed of Deuteronomy 6:4-9, 11:13-21, and Numbers 15:37-41. It begins as follows: "Hear (*shema*), O Israel: The LORD our God is *one* LORD!"

It is clear from the New Testament how well known these words were. Christ used them when He summarized the law (Mark 12:28ff), and we find allusions to them in many other places as well (see John 8:41; Rom. 3:30; Gal. 3:20; Eph. 4:6; I Tim. 2:5; James 2:19). The Lord is the one and only God. He will tolerate no Baals.

This makes a great deal of sense in the light of the central message and emphasis of Deuteronomy. Hear, O Israel! The Lord speaks through the service of His Word. Yahweh is one. He cannot be divided into a number of regional Baals.

A unique God. Yet there is more contained in this word *one*: not only is Yahweh the only God, He is also *unique*. His nature and revelation are unique. He, the Liberator and King of Israel, cannot be compared to the pseudo-liberators of the heathens.

> Thus says the LORD, the King of Israel
> and his Redeemer, the LORD of hosts:
> "I am the first and I am the last;
> besides me there is no god" (Is. 44:6).

Zechariah informs us: "And the LORD will become king over all the earth; on that day the LORD will be one and his name one" (Zech. 14:9).

It is not enough for us to be *monotheists*, confessing that there is but one God. The basic confession of the Muslims is that there is no God but Allah. Thus they, too, believe in *one* God. But that does not make their faith a true faith.

The God we must believe in is the God who has *revealed Himself in redemptive history*—in Egypt and on Golgotha. We must believe in the one and only Deliverer. There is no one else like Him. The church of the new covenant also proclaims: "Hear, O Israel: The Lord our God is one Lord. He is unique. You shall love the Lord your God."

From Deuteronomy 6 on, the Israelites are shown the many ways in which they must serve the one, unique God—or better: *may* serve. Little is left to the imagination.

God's sovereign will. Israël did not choose a god but was chosen by the Lord to be His people. But why did the Lord choose Israel? Was it because the Israelites were so *numerous?* "It was not because you were more in number than any other people that the LORD set his love upon you and chose you, for you were the fewest of all peoples" (7:7).

Was it because Israel was such a *powerful* nation? "Beware lest you say in your heart, 'My power and the might of my hand have gotten me this wealth.' You shall remember the LORD your God, for it is he who gives you power to get wealth" (8:17-18).

Was it perhaps because the Israelites were so *righteous* and *deserving*? "When the LORD your God drives them out before you, do not say to yourselves, 'It is because of my own merit that the LORD has brought me in to occupy this land.' Know then that it is not because of any merit of yours that the LORD your God is giving you this rich land to occupy; indeed, you are a stubborn people" (9:4, 6 NEB).

Why, then, was the LORD so gracious to Israel? "It is because the LORD loves you, and is keeping the oath which he swore to your fathers, that the LORD has brought you out with a mighty hand, and redeemed you from the house of bondage, from the hand of Pharaoh king of Egypt.

Know therefore that the LORD your God is God, the faithful God who keeps covenant and steadfast love with those who love him and keep his commandments, to a thousand generations" (7:8-9; see also 8:18; 9:5).

Here Moses is talking about the sovereignty of God's will. The Lord is a slave to His promised Word. He will always remember His redemptive purpose, the oath He swore to Abraham long ago, the unshakable covenant He made (see Luke 1:55, 73; 2:14).

Fearing the Lord. Yahweh tested His people to find out whether they really wished to serve Him (8:2ff), but the Israelites were stubborn (9:7ff). Moses points to a few specific incidents, such as the worship of the golden calf. But the Lord was always gracious. His everlasting grace is the basis of Israel's existence.

> And now, Israel, what does the LORD your God require of you, but to fear the LORD your God, to walk in all his ways, to love him, to serve the LORD your God with all your heart and with all your soul, and to keep the commandments and statutes of the LORD, which I command you this day for your good? Behold, to the LORD your God belong heaven and the heaven of heavens, the earth with all that is in it; yet the LORD set his heart in love upon your fathers and chose their descendants after them, you above all peoples, as at this day. Circumcise therefore the foreskin of your heart, and be no longer stubborn (10:12-16; see also Mic. 6:8; Jer. 4:4).

We must not be misled by the word *fear* in this passage. It does not mean being frightened of God in His sovereign will. Instead it involves taking Him into account, respecting Him, living by His torah. Deuteronomy is a continuous appeal to return Yahweh's love in a heartfelt way rather than just an external way.

If Israel will heed this appeal, the Lord will give His blessing. But if Israel is disobedient, the Lord will become angry. The people must choose between the path of blessing and the path of curse (ch. 11). That's why they were asked once more at Shechem to express their wishes clearly.

5. Concrete Covenant Demands

Covenant renewal. Because chapter 12 begins a new section of the book of Deuteronomy, I will pause briefly to sum up what we have established up to this point. We have seen that the book of Deuteronomy is *anti-Canaanite* in its overall thrust. It preaches Yahweh, the God who has freely chosen Israel as His inheritance.

This choice was a matter of His sovereign love; the stubborn Israelites did not become the object of His love on account of their own merits. In His great mercy, the Lord accepted the Israelites as His people and led them out of the house of bondage. He was faithful to the promises He had made to the patriarchs. At Sinai He renewed the covenant. After the long journey through the wilderness, the Sinai covenant was confirmed on the plains of Moab.

Deuteronomy gives us an introduction to this renewed covenant, a covenant calling for the people to return God's love with a total, all-embracing love of their own. The one, unique Lord demanded service in all areas of life.

Worship. The same emphases are present in the material that follows chapter 12, where they are applied to the central elements in Israel's life: worship (the *priestly* aspect), *prophecy,* and the courts (the *kingly* office). The anti-Canaanite emphasis also comes through here.

Heathendom, too, operates with mediators and office-bearers. Balaam, for example, was a priestly and prophetic figure. Those heathen office-bearers often had very high opinions of themselves and their positions. They claimed to have a special relationship with the gods and declared themselves inviolable.

This applied especially to the king. The king was a son of the gods. He ruled in an absolute way, as if he actually were a god. Heathendom is liberal in its recognition of numerous gods and deified people.

But *Yahweh* is *one*! (6:4). Therefore Israel was not to take over the Canaanite altars and places of worship. The cultic centers dedicated to the male Baals and female Astartes had to be destroyed. Only the place designated by the Lord could be used for offering sacrifices (ch. 12). And the Levites had to be accorded official recognition—in part through the giving of tithes (12:17ff).

Prophecy. The Israelites were instructed to listen critically to what was said by the "prophets" and by those who "dream dreams." If an alleged prophet urged the Israelites to serve other gods, his message was to be rejected. The Israelites were not to assume that whatever a prophet said must be true. The rule to be followed was that *every* purported revelation must be in harmony with *previous* revelations of the Lord.

Even if a "prophet" predicted some miraculous event as a sign of his calling and his prediction was borne out, this was still no indication that the Israelites were supposed to heed his appeal to serve other gods. Through such "prophets," the Lord would *test* His people from time to time to see whether they would be faithful to Him (13:1ff). Therefore the Israelites were always to compare a new prophecy with previous prophecies—and we should do the same. In I John 4:1 we read: "Beloved, do not believe every spirit, but test the spirits to see whether they are of God; for many false prophets have gone out into the world."

Israel had to be fully aware of the abiding danger of heathendom creeping into its worship by means of some "prophet," some preacher seeming to possess authority. Hence the false prophets were to be put to death (13:5) so that the evil would be removed from the midst of Israel. Paul speaks the same language when he discusses church *discipline*: wicked persons are to be "driven out" (I Cor. 5:13). In the New Testament, the death penalty is replaced by excommunication: the transgressor is to have no more contact with the congregation until he repents and turns to the Lord. It is clear from the rest of Deuteronomy 13 that discipline is to be applied whether the sin involves only a small circle of people (vs. 6-11) or is more public in nature (vs. 12-18).

Justice. Deuteronomy goes on to give further instructions about worship and the administration of justice. Here again we see the elements we noted earlier, namely, an *anti-heathen* emphasis and an accentuation of the significance of the *emancipation from Egypt.*

The instructions on justice manifest an eye for *social* considerations. We find a beautiful example of this social awareness in 15:7-11. The Israelites must be generous to the *poor*. All the Israelites together form a brotherhood, a community of people with obligations toward each other. The prospect of an approaching sabbath year in which debts would be forgiven automatically should not hold back anyone's generosity.

Furthermore, there was to be no bending or twisting of the law. Bribes were strictly forbidden. All persons appearing in court were to be treated alike by the judges. Later the prophets harped on the same point.

The rule requiring at least two or three witnesses, which we encounter in the New Testament (Matt. 18:16; John 5:32), is already to be found in Deuteronomy (see 17:6; 19:15). Thus no case could come to trial unless there were witnesses. Moreover, the witness bringing the accusation was to "cast the first stone" (17:7; see also John 8:7). Since he would be the one to carry out the sentence, he bore a heavy responsibility when he presented his testimony.

Military regulations. When we turn to the laws governing warfare, we see that considerable provision was made for exemptions from military service. We should also note that the enemy is to be offered peace terms *before* the attack (20:10).

In a demonstration of ecological concern, even the fruit trees are drawn into the instructions about warfare: they are not to be chopped down during a war. Thus, "scorched earth" tactics are forbidden (20:19).* When Elisha later advised the use of such tactics anyway, this was "false prophecy" on his part; the tactics did not lead to the desired results (see II Kings 3:19, 25-7).

The conduct of kings. In 17:14-20 we read some laws that have to do with the choice of a king and the conduct of kings. The king could not be a foreigner; he had to be one of the Israelites, chosen by God to serve as king.

We are then given a detailed portrait of the Messianic kingly ideal. Israel's ruler is not to compete with the surrounding heathen kings as though he were an autocrat or some sort of son of the gods. Definite restrictions were imposed on him. He was not to buy horses from Egypt, the land from which Israel had been liberated (see Is. 30:16; 31:1, and think of Solomon's stud farm). He was not to establish a great harem full of foreign princesses (think again of Solomon, who got into various difficulties because of all his wives), nor was he to set his heart on

---

*We should also note the concern for the bird in its nest, the ox treading on grain, and anyone who might happen to be walking from roof to roof (see 22:6-7; 25:4; 22:8). Ecology in the Bible!

heaping up riches for himself. The king was bound to the law of Moses and was not to elevate himself above his brothers. Like them, he was to listen to the prophets and bow before God's will as expressed in the torah.

In later history we see something of this kingly ideal exemplified. The king, as a man after God's own heart, is to treasure God's testimonies and seek guidance from the prophets. This "testimony" later played a role in the coronation ceremony (II Chron. 23:11). The king who was to foreshadow the coming Messiah would have to feel one with his brothers and separate from the nations and rulers living all around him; he would therefore have to live within the covenant made with Yahweh.

Fulfillment in Christ. Christ was the first King to fulfill all of this. He had no silver and no gold. He rode into Jerusalem on a donkey. He had come to do God's will in all things (Heb. 10:7). Wasn't He our High Priest and King?

That Christ was a prophet as well as a king is already indicated in 18:15: "The LORD your God will raise up for you a prophet like me from among you, for your brethren—him you shall heed" (18:15; see also John 6:14; Acts 3:22; 7:37; Matt. 17:5). The Jews condemned Christ as the false prophet of Deuteronomy 13, arguing that He deserved the death penalty, but the church may proclaim that He is the true prophet of Deuteronomy 18.

Bound to the Word. Deuteronomy 18 does not apply to Christ alone. The Lord means to say that since there will always be a prophet in Israel, there is no need to consult heathen soothsayers. In the words *your brothers*, by which the circle of the covenant people is meant, we hear the voice of Yahweh speaking to us through the prophet. Hear, O Israel!

That voice binds the people as well as the priests and

kings to the Word, the law that has been given. There is no room for manmade religion in Israel. Above Israel stands the Lord, who, as King, is the supreme lawgiver.

When the covenant was renewed on the plains of Moab, Moses, as prophet and mediator, declared: "This day you have become the people of the LORD your God. You shall therefore obey the voice of the LORD your God, keeping his commandments and his statutes, which I command you this day" (27:9-10).

A nation set apart. All the other incidental laws and regulations in chapters 18 through 26 should be viewed from this perspective. As a holy nation, Israel's feasts and public life would be subject to the laws of the God who decreed that Israel was to be a separate nation and was not to mingle with the pagans.

Israel was to be set apart not because it was somehow a better "race" than the other nations but because it had been chosen by the Lord to honor His name. Hear, O Israel!

6. The Covenant's Blessings, Curses and Witnesses

The opposite of shalom. What if the Israelites should refuse to listen? Moses decreed that the curses and blessings of the covenant were to be made known in the heart of Canaan: the curses at Mount Ebal, and the blessings at Mount Gerizim. It is striking how extensive the curses are (see ch. 27-28). The words of the covenant, of course, are also lengthy (ch. 29).

Echoes of these curses pronounced by Moses are to be found in the prophets. The gates of hell are opened in these curses, for they represent the exact opposite of shalom or peace (29:19). The destruction of Jerusalem, which took place twice in history, is already mentioned in this series of curses.

Creation as a witness. Moses points out that repentance will lead to forgiveness and blessing (30:1-10), but such repentance must include a willingness to listen to the voice of the Lord. That His voice should continue to be heard is a matter of great grace on God's part. Prophecy will not die out, the Israelites are assured. There is no need to cross vast seas or ascend to heaven to hear the Word of the Lord. "The word is very near you; it is in your mouth and in your heart" (30:11-14; see also Rom. 10:6-10).

The exhortation "Hear, O Israel" remains a rule for the church. Faith is a matter of listening, but it is also a matter of grace. What we must listen to is the preaching of the Word. "I call heaven and earth to witness against you this day, that I have set before you life and death, blessing and curse; therefore choose life, that you and your descendants may live, loving the Lord your God, obeying his voice, and cleaving to him; for that means life to you" (30:19-20).

Just as a covenant between a suzerain king and his vassals required witnesses, the Lord here appeals to the *creation* as His witness. The Word is near you (Ps. 19). The spacious firmament is an accusing witness when the covenant is broken (Rom. 10:18, 8).

The song of Moses. In case of rebellion on man's part, there was another witness that would make itself heard, namely, a song impressed upon the minds of all the members of the covenant. The theme of this song of Moses is: "A God of *faithfulness* and without iniquity, *just* and *right* is he" (32:4).

Yahweh was good to Israel. He carried Israel as an eagle carries its young (32:6-14; see also Rev. 4:7; 12:14). But were the Israelites thankful to the Lord? No, they returned *evil* for *good* (32:5-6, 15-18). Referring to Israel by the poetic name *Jeshurun*, Moses declares:

> But Jeshurun waxed fat, and kicked;
> you waxed fat, you grew thick, you became sleek;
> then he forsook God who made him,
> and scoffed at the Rock of his salvation (32:15).

Thus Jeshurun did not live up to his beautiful name, which seems to be related to the word *upright*. This aroused the Lord's wrath (32:19ff), for He had declared long before that He would not tolerate such flagrant wickedness as Israel's idolatry. He would have wiped out the Israelites completely by means of their enemies, but those enemies would then have drawn the conclusion that Yahweh was *powerless* to protect His people (32:26-31).

The antithesis within Israel. As for the later verses (vs. 32ff) in the song of Moses, the disagreement about their meaning goes all the way back to the Jewish rabbis. Some believed that God was still talking about the pagans and threatening them with judgment. Others believed that God was referring to apostate Israel, declaring that Israel would not escape punishment.

I accept the latter interpretation. *Within Israel* there would be an *antithesis*, an *opposition*, between those who were *faithful* and those who *fell* away. But the Lord would vindicate His people and deal justly with them (32:36); He would have mercy on His servants and avenge them (vs. 43). He *is*, and there is no other besides Him. He kills and makes alive; He wounds and heals (vs. 39). In New Testament language, we would say that Christ preserves His Church even against the combined forces of hell.

Echoes of Moses' song. Later Israelites used this song of Moses regularly in the temple services. Therefore it became very familiar. In one of the caves by the Dead Sea, a fragment of a separate copy of this song was found. It should not surprise us, then, that we find various allusions to this song in the Old Testament as well as the New.

As you read this song, you will probably notice that the Lord is repeatedly referred to by the strange name *Rock*. This comforting image of God also appears in the book of Psalms (see, for example, Ps. 18:2; 19:14; 31:3; 71:3; 92:15; 94:22). The name *Jeshurun* occurs again in the book of Isaiah (see Is. 44:1), which also quotes part of 32:39.* The words "Vengeance is mine, and recompense" (32:35) are quoted repeatedly in the Bible (see Rom. 12:19 and Heb. 10:30, where Deut. 32:36 is also cited.) Finally, in the book of Revelation we find a number of cries that reflect either the theme of the song of Moses (32:4) or its conclusion (vs. 43).†

---

*Is. 43:10ff. Compare Deut. 32:39 with I Sam. 2:6 (the song of Hanna); Hos. 6:1-2; Matt. 16:21; Luke 24:26-7, 44; John 5:21; Rom. 4:17; 8:11; II Cor. 1:9; 13:4; I Tim. 6:13; I Pet. 3:18; Rev. 1:18.

†Deut. 32:4 is quoted in Rev. 15:3; 16:7; 19:2. Deut. 32:43 is echoed in Rev. 6:10; 16:5-6; 18:20; 19:2. There are more places in the New Testament that draw on Deuteronomy 32: for example, compare Matt. 11:16; 12:39, 41; 16:4; 17:17; 23:36; 24:34; Acts 2:40; and Phil. 2:15 with Deut. 32:5, 20, where Moses speaks of a "perverse generation."

The Old Testament includes a number of songs in addition to the Psalms. Both the synagogue and the early Christian church made good use of them. The Roman Catholics still give these songs some liturgical recognition. The Protestant churches did not restore these songs to the liturgy, despite the fact that Marnix and Beza prepared rhymed versions of them. Many of these songs do not fit the tastes of a generation that would rather sing of a "loving" God than of a covenant God who can become very angry.

The Christian churches would do well to break with this self-imposed poverty and return to the practice of the synagogue and the early church by using these songs in their worship services. There are certainly some hymns in our hymnbooks that we could do without. Perhaps we should replace them with these Old Testament songs. If we did so, we would no longer be disobedient with regard to God's command about Moses' last song (see Deut. 31:19, 21-2, 28, 30; 32:44ff; Rev. 15:3).

When we bear in mind that the "enemies" mentioned in this song are not just heathen opponents but also *apostates within the church*, we can see what comfort the song of Moses has provided the faithful Israelites of the old covenant as well as the new. The Lord will avenge the blood of His servants. The faithful God of the covenant will uphold His church.

A blessing on Israel. The blessing given by Moses (Deut. 33) should be compared with Jacob's blessing (Gen. 49). We see that *Simeon* is not mentioned. (This tribe was given certain cities in Judah's territory.) Moreover, this time the priestly tribe of Levi, which had firmly resisted apostasy, is not cursed (see Gen. 49:5-7) but *blessed* (see Num. 25:6-13; Mal. 2:5-7; Jer. 33:19-22). Moses speaks at length about Ephraim and Manasseh, the sons of Joseph.

At the beginning of the blessing, an appearance of the Lord is sketched in powerful words (see Ps. 68 and Hab. 3). At the end comes a prophetic doxology:

> There is none like God, O Jeshurun,
> who rides through the heavens to your help,
> and in his majesty through the skies.
> The eternal God is your dwelling place,
> and underneath are the everlasting arms.
> Happy are you, O Israel! Who is like you,
> a people saved by the LORD,
> the shield of your help,
> and the sword of your triumph!
> Your enemies shall come fawning to you;
> and you shall tread upon their high places (33:26-7, 29).

The death of Israel's leader. Deuteronomy ends with an account of Moses' death. Of course Moses did not write this section of Scripture himself; the record of this event must have been composed later.

We sense a definite yearning when we read the declaration that there has never been such a prophet again since the time of Moses (34:10ff). There is a longing for the old days, but also a Messianic yearning for the coming of the One who will be greater than Moses and will serve as Mediator of the new covenant.

We should also note that the leadership succession is dealt with explicitly at the end of the book. We are told that the people did indeed follow the successor designated by Moses—Joshua. Because of the laying on of hands, this successor was full of the Spirit of wisdom. (The Revised Standard Version does not use a capital letter here for *Spirit.)*

Regardless of who the office-bearers in the church may be and regardless of how they may differ in gifts and abilities, obedience to the covenant means standing by the faithful and lawful office-bearers of the covenant and respecting the covenant's organs and institutions. As far as this point is concerned, there is no difference between "Mosaic" and "apostolic" succession. (As you ponder this matter, read Acts 20:24ff and II Timothy 1:6-7.) We are to take good care of what has been entrusted to us.

Joshua

Thanks be to God, who gives us the victory through our Lord Jesus Christ (I Cor. 15:57).

1. Main Themes

The conquest of the promised land. The book of Joshua can be characterized as the book of the Lord's wars. It describes the conquest of the land of promise. The oath sworn to Abraham was no idle promise: after Abraham became a great *nation* (the people of Israel), he also received a *land* (Canaan). This was a matter of God's free grace.

When Joshua, at the end of his life, pleaded with the people to remain faithful to Yahweh, he reminded them that their fathers had long ago served other gods when they lived beyond the Euphrates (24:2, 14ff; see also Deut. 26:5ff). It was only because of God's sovereign grace that Abram was called and Israel was brought into Canaan.

The book of Joshua makes it abundantly clear that Abraham's descendants did not take possession of the promised land because of their own strength. It was always *the Lord* who gave them the victory.

Israel's leader. Joshua may have been a great general and military strategist, but he was always dependent on the One who fulfills His promises. The book of Joshua does not hide Joshua's faults.

As we read between the lines, we sense a yearning for the One who would lead the people to perfect "rest" and fullness of life. This Deliverer bore the same name as Moses' successor: He was Joshua of Nazareth. (*Jesus* is an Aramaic version of the Hebrew name *Joshua.*) *He* was the One who made possible the sabbath rest for which the people of God had been waiting (Heb. 3:7—4:11).

When thou didst go forth before thy people . . . (Ps. 68:7).

2. Securing a Foothold in Canaan

God's grace at work. The first chapters of the book of Joshua show us the free and mighty grace of God at work. The Lord gave Joshua the great promise that we hear so often in Scripture: "I will be *with you*" (1:5, 9). Joshua announced to the people that the time had come to cross the Jordan. But first he sent out spies.

In the city of Jericho, which was central to Canaan's defense, the spies enlisted the help of a fallen woman named Rahab. This woman not only hid them from the authorities but also testified of her faith, declaring that Israel's God would be victorious. He is not a local deity, she declared, but a universal God who showed through the wonders He performed in Egypt that He is greater than any other.

In the face of Jericho's crisis, Rahab now sought refuge in this God. The spies assured her that because of her faithfulness, she and her family would be spared when the city was taken. Thus this woman was incorporated into Israel in a wonderful way; among her descendants were David and Jesus (see Matt. 1:5ff).

The very beginning of the book of Joshua, which is so full of the judgment of God on the Canaanites, presents this beautiful story of the grace shown to a daughter of degenerate Canaan. Although she had grown up *outside* the "church," there was salvation for her!

A path through the Jordan. The spies came back with a triumphant report. Rahab had told them that the inhabitants of Jericho trembled in fear of the Israelites. It was time to cross the Jordan!

The ark (the symbol of the Lord's throne) was first in the procession. The God who had dried up the Red Sea so that the Israelites could pass through was still with them: He made a path through the waters of the Jordan as well. He may have done so through natural means, but this does not make it any less a miracle.

Joshua saw to it that a pioneer monument was erected at Gilgal, the first resting point. The monument was made of twelve stones taken from the Jordan's riverbed.

The book of Joshua could well be called the "book of the speaking stones." Later in the book we will encounter more monuments. These stones served as a children's Bible—or better: a catechism. They were intended to encourage the children to ask questions. The parents would answer by telling them about the wondrous deeds of Yahweh (4:4ff, 20ff).

Circumcision and the Passover. Before the Israelites could proceed with the attack on Jericho, there was something important to be done. All the male Israelites were to be circumcised. During the journey through the wilderness (which most Israelites regarded as a death march, a curse), the practice of circumcision had been dropped.

The Passover was also celebrated. This had important implications for future Passover celebrations. From then on the Passover would not just be a reminder of the exodus from Egypt but also a way of remembering the crossing of the Jordan and the entry into Canaan.

Israel crossed the Jordan four days before the day of the Passover, on the day when the Passover lamb was to be *selected* (see 4:19; see also Ex. 12:3). The Passover—think of Jesus Christ—speaks not only of a departure but also of an arrival!

A divine battle plan. Just as we read in Exodus about Moses and the burning bush, there is an extraordinary phenomenon recorded in Joshua. Israel's new leader encountered a commander of the army of the Lord—an angel with a drawn sword. Like Moses, Joshua was ordered to take off his shoes, for he was on holy ground. The angel assured him that Jericho would fall to the Israelites. Joshua was also told what military measures to employ.

The plan was a strange one. For six days in succession, the Israelite warriors would march once around the city without making any noise. On each occasion they were to be followed by seven priests blowing trumpets, and also by the ark, the throne of God. On the seventh day they were to march around the city seven times, again with the priests blowing their trumpets. Then, when a great cry issued from all the people, the walls of the city would collapse and the city could be taken.

That was the angel's plan of attack. Joshua carried out the plan just as he was told. The city did indeed fall and was completely destroyed.

Jericho was to remain a pile of ruins indefinitely, as a monument to warn the Israelites: "Be careful that this doesn't happen to you" (see 6:26). Anyone who rebuilt the city would be cursed. In the days of King Ahab, Hiel of Bethel rebuilt the city—at the cost of his oldest and youngest sons (I Kings 16:34).

Drive out the wicked person from among you (I Cor. 5:13).

3. A Curse in the Camp

Achan's sin. Time and again the Bible speaks of apostasy within the church. This motif already occurs in the book of Joshua, where we meet Achan, who kept some of Jericho's treasures for himself contrary to the Lord's express orders.

As punishment for this deed, the Israelites lost a battle against the city of Ai. (*Ai,* which may well be a later name, means *heap of ruins.*) The Lord informed Joshua that the Israelites' defeat was due to the presence of a transgressor in their midst. By lot it was determined that Achan was the guilty party. He confessed and was stoned to death with his family and household.

A "troubler of Israel." Using Achan's name in a pun, Joshua asked him why he had brought trouble upon the people of Israel. (*Aakar* means: bring trouble.) A great heap of stones was set up in the valley where he was stoned—another monument! This valley was named the Valley of Achor (i.e. valley of troubles, misfortune). In I Chronicles 2:7, Achan is referred to as the "troubler of Israel"; he is the man who plunged Israel into defeat. King Ahab applied this name to Elijah during the great drought (see I Kings 18:17).

Because those who prefer old-fashioned Scriptural language sometimes use the term *troubler of Israel* to refer to someone who gets things going or livens things up, we must be aware of the real meaning and background of this expression. It is a very serious matter to be a "troubler of Israel." Achan's sin led to the punishment of the whole congregation. Even today the church regards this event as a reason to insist on the maintenance of church discipline.

Otherwise God's wrath would be directed against the whole congregation (see Answer 82 of the Heidelberg Catechism).

A door of hope. The Valley of Achor was mentioned by the prophets much later in Israel's history (see Is. 65:10; Hos. 2:15). But to their way of thinking, this episode is not all darkness. The entryway to Canaan is no longer a gateway to unhappiness but a door of hope. It is Christ who makes this perspective possible. It is through His subjection to punishment and the curse that we are saved.

The city of Ai was also punished when it was finally captured after Achan's death. The king of Ai was hanged on a tree. His body was taken down in the evening, in accordance with the law recorded in Deuteronomy 21:23. Anyone who is hanged is accursed by God. This reminds us at once of Christ's death on the cross. Our Savior was "elevated," just as this Canaanite king was elevated. He, too, was cursed (see Josh. 8:29; 10:26ff; John 19:31; Gal. 3:13). He became someone who defiled the land—so that *we* could inherit "the land," the blessed earth.

to your descendants I will give this land (Gen. 12:7).

4. Completing the Conquest

Shechem. In Joshua 8:30ff, we read how Joshua built an altar at Shechem, the center of the land, and then read aloud the covenant's provisions about blessings and curses (see also Deut. 11:29; 27:12-13). In the heart of Canaan, where Abram first heard the promise (Gen. 12:7), the Word of the One who demands Israel's heart was heard.

We can well understand why Joshua also chose Shechem

for his *parting address* to the Israelites. Once more the voice of the covenant was heard in Shechem at an assembly of the people.

The Gibeonites. Joshua and the other leaders certainly did not take the proper position in the matter of the Gibeonites (one of the Canaanite peoples). The law, the pact with King Yahweh (of which Joshua had just reminded the people), expressly forbade the Israelites to make any treaty or alliance with a foreign nation.

Joshua found himself faced with emissaries claiming to come from a faraway land. In fact, however, they represented a nation in the midst of Canaan. These emissaries exemplified the old proverb "Necessity is the mother of invention." If the Israelites were too strong for them, they would have to be defeated by cunning rather than force.

Unfortunately, Joshua did not seek the Lord's advice in this matter. He was flattered by the words of the emissaries and made a covenant with them. Later he found out that he had been deceived, but he had to abide by the oath he had sworn (ch. 9). Thus Gibeon was spared. To neutralize the evil influence that these Canaanites would be sure to have on Israel, the Gibeonites were made to serve in the house of the Lord (vs. 27).

A coalition in the south. In the south of Canaan, a coalition of five kings was formed. We can well understand that these kings would feel compelled to attack the Gibeonites, for when the Gibeonites made a covenant with the Israelites, they left a dangerous gap in the Canaanite line of defense.

Israel came to Gibeon's assistance, and the five allied kings were defeated. On that day Joshua spoke the famous words: "Sun, stand thou still at Gibeon, and thou Moon in the valley of Aijalon" (10:12). When evening came, there was still daylight (see Zech. 14:7; Rev. 22:5).

Nature seemed to be intensely involved in the struggle of the Church. Wasn't the creation cursed together with man? Isn't the creation yearning for the great re-creation, when man and the creation will together be glorified? (Rom. 8:19-23). Then night will no longer be an obstacle. The wonderful extension of the daylight during the battle of Gibeon was a prophetic indication of what is to come.

A coalition in the north. After the south was conquered and its fortresses captured one by one, the Israelites turned to the north. There, too, a coalition had been formed. But in the battle at the waters of Merom, this coalition was routed.

We read that the northern allies had many horses and chariots, which leads us to suppose that their army must have been very strong. But Joshua had received an assurance from the Lord that the Israelites would triumph. He was commanded to burn all the chariots and make the horses lame by hamstringing them (11:6).

This command must be viewed in the light of one of the laws governing the conduct of kings (Deut. 17:16). The Israelites were not to trust in the military methods and tools of the pagans; instead, they were to live in complete dependence on the Lord. Hence we read in a "battle prayer" in one of the psalms: "Some boast of chariots, and some of horses; but we boast of the name of the LORD our God" (Ps. 20:7).

Cities built on ruins. As we read Joshua 11, we must focus our attention on another decree by which the Lord hoped to teach Israel humility. We read that Israel did not burn the cities that "stood on mounds," except for Hazor. We might wonder why these cities were not burned. The answer is that the mounds on which they were built were composed of ruins. Although the newer cities were burned, the Israelites were not required to burn the cities that had already been destroyed earlier in history.

The intent was that each of the cities of the Israelites would be built on top of ruins. This would be a warning to the Israelites that if they did not stay away from the sins of the Canaanites, their cities would wind up as piles of ruins too. If the Israelites served the Baals, they would lay themselves open to the same judgment as the Canaanites. Our God is a consuming fire.

Dividing the land. In the section on the division of the land (13:1-7), mention is made of territories that had not yet been conquered. The land divided up between the various tribes had not been completely purified of enemy military forces yet. The power of the enemy had indeed been broken, but the last resistance would have to be overcome in mopping-up operations.

Reuben, Gad, and half of the tribe of Manasseh were granted land beyond the Jordan. Caleb, the spy who (together with Joshua) had earlier submitted a minority report in favor of invading Canaan, was given Hebron as his inheritance (14:6-15). Hebron was the area where the dreaded giants lived. That Caleb desired just this piece of land, which would be hard to conquer, illustrates the power of his faith (14:12). In chapter 15 we read about the inheritance of Judah, and in the following two chapters about the inheritance of the two tribes of Joseph (Ephraim and Manasseh). These three were the largest tribes. They were to play a dominant role in Israel's history.

The tabernacle was erected at Shiloh. There the remaining seven tribes were informed what land they would receive. The tribe of Levi, of course, received a special inheritance—the priesthood of the Lord (18:7; see also Deut. 18:2).

A commission of 21 men was established to survey and describe the rest of the land so that it could be divided. The

Israelites had delayed long enough in taking possession of the land of promise. The time had come to seize the prize.

We sense that the tribes were somewhat hesitant about proceeding. Was this a premonition of the later apostasy? In any event, Joshua went ahead. Once the commission had completed its work, he cast lots in the presence of the Lord to assign the various territories to the tribes (18:8ff).

Joshua himself received an inheritance in the hill country of Ephraim (19:49-51). Cities were assigned to the Levites, and some of them were designated as cities of refuge (ch. 20-21). The chronicle concludes fittingly by pointing out: "Thus the LORD gave to Israel *all the land* which he swore to give to their fathers. Not one of all the good promises which the LORD had made to the house of Israel had failed; all came to pass" (21:43, 45).

A land of milk and honey. In the light of this faithfulness on God's part, we see why the book of Joshua includes the names of so many cities and territories. The passages with all the names are not the ones we should be reading aloud at the table after the evening meal. (In earlier generations, such passages were sometimes used to give children practice in reading aloud!) The names were not included in the Bible to provide us with tongue-twisters; rather, they are a concrete illustration of God's *faithfulness.*

The lists of cities give us reason to rejoice. The Lord "gave their land as a heritage, for his steadfast love endures for ever" (Ps. 136:21). If you open your Bible atlas at a map of Israel at the time of the conquest of Canaan, you can read all these place names in their geographical setting. The fulfillment of the promise is reflected even in the meaning of the names!

Israel's new home was truly a land of milk and honey. It included such towns as Bethlehem (place of food), Rimmon (pomegranate), Gath-hepher (wine press of the well),

Jabneel (God is builder), Naamah (pleasant), Tappuah (apple tree), Beeroth (wells), and Irpeel (God heals). Israel's feeling of being at home is expressed in such names as Shamir (thorn hedge), Shaalabbin (jackals), and Socoh (enclosure of thorns). Sin's consequences had not yet vanished!

All these names must be viewed in the light of the great theme of Joshua—the grace of Israel's covenant God. These names point to the great Joshua, the Messiah who has won an eternal, perfect inheritance for us. Through Him, our lot or inheritance is established in the heavens. The Spirit is a guarantee of our inheritance until we take full possession of it (Eph. 1:11, 14).

If Joshua had given them rest . . . (Heb. 4:8).

5. The Last Days of Joshua

The threat of apostasy. The book of Joshua sketches the dangers of apostasy in clear terms. Think of the story of Achan, for example. Here and there we are shown that the Israelites were not as faithful as they should have been when it came to driving all the Canaanites out of the land (see 16:10; 17:12ff; 18:3). The story of the altar by the Jordan shows us that apostasy or turning away from the Lord was already considered a definite danger.

Before the people of Gad, Reuben and half the tribe of Manasseh crossed the Jordan to take possession of the land assigned to them as their inheritance, they built a great altar. When the other tribes found out, they regarded this deed as an act of unfaithfulness to the Lord. If it really was a case of apostasy, they would have to bring the provisions of Deuteronomy 12 and 13 into play and punish the wayward tribes. Therefore there was a sudden mobilization of soldiers at Shiloh.

Fortunately, the Israelites were wise enough to stop and think for a moment before attacking. Phinehas, who had already distinguished himself in his zeal for the Lord at Baal-peor, was first sent with a delegation to the suspect tribes to ask what the building of the altar meant. As he addressed the two and a half tribes, he reminded them of the sin at Baal-peor and the curse that had struck all the Israelites after Achan's sin. Were the two and a half tribes perhaps dissatisfied with the land assigned to them? Was their land unclean? Why did they have to build an altar before they crossed the Jordan? Surely this was an instance of manmade religion, which could lead to all sorts of misfortune!

The two and a half tribes answered that the altar was intended as a *monument* to remind later generations that the tribes across the Jordan were one with the rest of Israel in "church" and worship. The altar was never intended to be used for offerings. Thus there had been a grave misunderstanding. The altar, which was just like the one at Shiloh, had been erected as a symbol of unity. After this explanation, there was no more talk of war and punishment (ch. 22).

An echo of Moses. The danger of unfaithfulness to the covenant was always there, if only in latent form. When aged Joshua, who had withdrawn to his homestead in the hill country of Ephraim, felt the end approaching, he called Israel's office-bearers together. (We are not told where.) To these leaders he again emphasized that what the Lord required of them was faithfulness to the law of Moses—and especially no fraternizing with the Canaanites. On the contrary, the remaining Canaanites must be wiped out.

There was to be no thought of Israel imitating even the

style of Baal worship. Just as the Lord was faithful in fulfilling His promises, He would be faithful in venting His wrath if the covenant was broken (ch. 24). Moses' words of farewell in Deuteronomy are echoed in Joshua's final words to his "church council."

Covenant renewal. Just as Moses renewed the covenant with the Lord in the fields of Moab, Joshua saw to it that the covenant was confirmed before he died. This event took place at Shechem, the very center of the land.

Earlier Shechem had been a bulwark of Canaanite power. It was also the place where the Lord first promised Abram that his descendants would receive "this land" (Gen. 12:7). And it was the place where Simeon and Levi played their shameful trick on the men involved in dishonoring their sister Dinah. (They asked that the men be circumcised and then took advantage of their temporary incapacity to kill them.) Finally, Shechem was the place where Jacob buried his idols before he went to Bethel (Gen. 34 and 35:1-4).

Joshua's parting words. It was not without reason that Joshua began his address at Shechem by reminding the Israelites of the patriarchs. Were their gods not buried under the terebinth at Shechem? "Thus says the LORD, the God of Israel, 'Your fathers lived of old beyond the Euphrates, Terah, the father of Abraham and of Nahor; and they served other gods. Then I took your father Abraham from beyond the River [i.e. the Euphrates] and led him through all the land of Canaan" (24:2-3).

Here the grace motif comes to the fore again. Joshua is speaking of the Lord's sovereign grace, which never lets us down if we live by the Bible.

In a few words Joshua reviews what the Lord has done for the Israelites, how He has led them out of Egypt and into the promised land. "I gave you a land on which you had not labored, and cities which you had not built, and you dwell therein; you eat the fruit of vineyards and olive yards which you did not plant" (24:13). There is no room for boasting, then.

Because of this rich background, the question of *commitment* is all the more important. What do the Israelites want? Do they want to worship the Mesopotamian gods that their fathers used to worship, the gods that even Jacob tolerated in his household before Shechem? Do they want to worship the Baals and Astartes of the Canaanites? Or do they wish to give their whole hearts to the Lord? Joshua knew what he wanted. "As for me and my house, we will serve the LORD" (24:15).

Israel's response. The people answered that they would not forsake the Lord. After all, it was the Lord who delivered them with a mighty hand. But Joshua did not want them to make a hasty choice. Were they aware that Yahweh is a jealous God? He would surely punish any breach of the covenant. The good gifts He had given them in the *past* were no guarantee that He would continue to be so merciful and generous in the *future*. There was also His covenant wrath to consider.

The people continued to insist that they would be faithful to the Lord. Joshua then declared himself a witness to their declaration and set up a great stone to serve as a silent witness of the renewed covenant. "It shall be a witness against you, lest you deal falsely with your God" (24:27).

Burial notices. The book of Joshua ends in a somber way. Joshua died shortly after the people at Shechem renewed the covenant. We are also told about the burial of the bones of Joseph and the death of Phinehas, the high priest.

The sounds we hear at the end of the book are not just lamentation. Joshua is also called the "servant of the

LORD," a title that Moses received and that Christ was later to bear. Joshua was buried on his own land, we are told. Joseph and Phinehas were also buried in their own territory. Here we see the Lord's faithfulness in fulfilling His *promises* to those who were faithful to Him. Yahweh is a God not of the dead but of the living (Mark 12:27).

In these burial notices, the trumpet of life sounds a note of triumph. The book of Joshua can finally come to an end. Yahweh is a God who keeps His promises.

Judges

[They] turned away and acted treacherously like their fathers (Ps. 78:57).

1. Turning Away from the Lord

Two introductions. Judges has *two* introductions (1:1—2:5 and 2:6—3:4). Then comes the main body of the book (3:5—16:31), which tells us about the various judges. Finally, there are two appendixes presenting us with a cross section of life in the time of the judges (ch. 17-18 and 19-21). The era is sketched for us by way of some typical events.

The introductions give us a clear picture of the situation. As long as Joshua and his elders were still alive, the Israelites continued to serve the Lord (Josh. 24:31; Judges 2:7). After Joshua was gone, however, they began to turn away from the Lord.

Agricultural gods. The Israelites had been nomads, but now they became a nation of farmers. To be sure of success in farming, they felt they should follow the lead of the

Canaanites and seek the favor of the agricultural gods. They did not propose to abandon Yahweh completely; they would simply worship other gods in addition. After all, each "god" would have to watch over his own domain.

Yahweh was clearly a great god of war, for He had led them in days of battle. But when it came to agriculture, wouldn't it be wiser to call on the male and female gods of the Canaanites, that is, the Baals and Astartes? They were the gods to see to it that the ground was fruitful. The sexual union of these male and female divinities would guarantee the fertility of the land. This sexual union should therefore be imitated in the worship services in the sanctuaries, through ceremonies involving the sacred pillars and poles.

Baal was the god of weather and rain, while Astarte (Mother Earth) was the goddess of fertility and sex. Many a place had its own Baal or its own Astarte (the Canaanite Venus and Madonna). Baal was "our dear Lord"—*Baal* means *lord*—and Astarte "our beloved Lady."

Contact with the Canaanites. Judges 1 shows us that wars of conquest were still being fought, although many of the tribes neglected the task of eliminating the foreign element in Canaan. What was worse was that the Israelites began intermarrying with the Canaanites. Instead of *antithesis*, then, there was *synthesis*.

The covenant was neglected (2:1-3), which aroused the Lord's wrath. Enemies invaded the land, and the Israelites soon had to ask for the Lord's help. He gave them judges who delivered them from the attacks of the neighboring nations and hostile nomads. But before long, the danger would be forgotten and the people would fall back into the same sins again. In the stories about the judges we find a monotonous cycle: apostasy, judgment sent by the Lord, repentance, deliverance by a judge, and more apostasy.

The judges. When we hear the word *judge*, we think of someone presiding over a court. In the Old Testament, however, the word has a broader meaning: a judge can also be active on the battlefield. Judging often means seeing to it that *justice is done.* A judge, then, is someone who *delivers* his people and executes judgment on the enemy.

The book of Judges shows us how the Lord, during Israel's dark middle ages, repeatedly called individuals to the office of judge, anointed them with His Spirit, and had them fight the Lord's wars. Because there was little unity among the tribes in those days—apostasy was fragmenting the nation—the judges sometimes worked within the framework of a single tribe. There was no succession among them, and the good they did rarely endured after their passing (2:19).

This made the necessity of kingly rule increasingly clear. The period of the judges cried out for a king—indeed, for *the* King, Jesus Christ, who brings complete justice for His people, defending them and keeping them safe from all their enemies. He is the Judge who truly saves (see Lord's Day 19 of the Heidelberg Catechism).

Israel's enemies. If you survey the deeds of the various judges, you will see what a series of enemies the Israelites faced: Othniel (the Mesopotamians), Ehud (the Moabites), Shamgar (the Philistines), Barak (the Canaanites), Gideon (nomadic Amalekites and Midianites), Jephthah (the Ammonites), and Samson (the Philistines). Open your Bible atlas to see where all these people lived, and you will quickly realize that the Israelites were given little peace by the nations living around them.

The Israelites could not afford to relax in the midst of their vineyards and fig trees. Here, too, we hear the cry for a Messianic King who would provide true "rest" and safety (see Matt. 11:28-9; see also Is. 28:12; Jer. 16:6; Heb. 4:8-11).

The spirit of the times. The accounts of the lives and deeds of the judges show us that the judges themselves were influenced by the spirit of the times. They were human beings subject to the usual shortcomings and failings. Barak was afraid (4:8). Gideon, after the incredible victory that went down in history as the "day of Midian" (see Is. 9:4; 10:26), fell into the sin of manmade religion: he ordered an ephod for himself, i.e. a priestly breastplate decorated with precious stones (8:22ff). Through this sin, he led Israel down the dangerous path of apostasy. His son Abimelech was proclaimed king at Shechem, the place where the covenant had last been renewed under Joshua!

It even turned out that the sanctuary there came to be devoted to the service of a foreign god, Baal-berith (i.e. the Baal or lord of the covenant). Abimelech used the temple treasures at Shechem to pay his band of followers to kill his brothers. This paved the way for him to become king. But his "kingship" was a failure, and he died an ignoble death (ch. 9; see also II Sam. 11:21).

When it comes to Jephthah, who had grown up outside the covenant circle, it could well be asked whether he was not too quick in making his vow. Furthermore, it appears that he had picked up a few heathen notions about winning the favor of the gods (11:30ff). And then there was Samson! He was a Nazirite dedicated to God, but Judges shows how far he fell (ch. 16).

Those who say, "As thy god lives, O Dan" (Amos 8:14).

2. Dan's Self-willed Worship

Micah's private sanctuary. The final chapters of the book of Judges underscore the degeneration of Israel. A certain Micah, who lived in the hill country of Ephraim, established his own private sanctuary, complete with an ephod and teraphim (household idols). By way of explanation, the writer of the book of Judges adds: "In those days there was *no king* in Israel; every man did what was *right in his own eyes*" (17:6). This statement occurs repeatedly in the later chapters (18:1; 19:1; 21:25). The writer points out time and again that such episodes cry out for a king who would rule in the name of the Lord.

What happened with Micah's little temple? He hired an "unemployed" Levite to serve as his priest (17:7ff). The arrangement was discovered by spies from the tribe of Dan. This tribe was already finding its assigned territory too small (1:34) and was seeking to expand its inheritance (18:1ff). When members of this tribe later passed the house of Micah in the course of their migration, they took the priest, who happened to be a grandson of Moses (see 18:30) with them. They also took along Micah's sacred objects.

A holy place in Dan. Once the migrating Danites settled down in the northernmost part of Canaan, they used the priest and his "equipment" to establish a holy place of their own in their new city, which they named *Dan* (18:30-1). This illegitimate worship center seems to have flourished for a long time. When King Jeroboam set up his calf worship in Bethel, he also set up a calf to be worshiped at Dan, apparently incorporating Dan's worship tradition into his new state religion (I Kings 12:28-9).

Clearly it was *not* Micah's intention to break completely with the service of the Lord; the money which he used to establish his own sanctuary and hire his own priest had been consecrated to the LORD (17:3). Yet, despite the good intentions, Micah and his mother were in fact transgressing the second commandment, which forbids worshiping images and devising any manmade religion. And sinning against the second commandment can easily lead to transgressions against the first. Think of the Roman Catholics.

From the days of Gibeah, you have sinned, O Israel (Hosea 10:9).

3. Punishing Benjamin

The Levite's concubine. In chapters 19-21 we are given a further indication of the ethical degeneration of Israel and its accommodation to Canaanite ways. Without attempting to mask the ugly facts, the writer tells us of conditions in the city of Gibeah, in Benjamin—where King Saul was later to be born! We are also given a portrait of a certain Levite and his concubine, a portrait not flattering to the Levite. At the time of this episode, the tribes still appeared to be fairly unified.

What happened was that the men of Gibeah wanted to sexually abuse the Levite, but settled for his concubine, whom they raped and left to die. Because the tribe of Benjamin chose to defend the men of Gibeah against the wrath of the other tribes this sorry episode led to a civil war.

After the Lord was consulted in Bethel (20:18), which was the resting place of the ark and the place where Jacob had his dream about the angels on the ladder, Benjamin was attacked. Twice the Benjaminites beat back the attack. The third time they were defeated through a trick. Then the entire tribe was punished for the atrocity committed by the men of Gibeah. Eventually there were only 600 men left.

Wives for the Benjaminites. Because the men of Israel had sworn not to give their daughters in marriage to the Benjaminites, it appeared that the tribe was doomed to disappear. We read of complaints raised to the Lord at Bethel, but we do not read that the Lord was *consulted* about the impasse. The Israelites sought a solution on their own—and found one.

The town of Jabesh-gilead had not sent any men when the mobilization took place. The Israelites would now wipe out the men of that town but spare the young virgins to be wives for the Benjaminites.* When this procedure did not yield enough wives, the feast at Shiloh was raided and more prospective wives were seized. A feast of the Lord (perhaps a Passover) was violated so that the Israelites could live up to their oath!

Self-righteousness. What strikes us immediately about this disgraceful train of events is that the people seemed to approach the keeping of the Lord's ordinances in a thoroughly formalistic and superficial manner. First they could not see past the black sin of the Benjaminites—as though there were no grave sinners in their own ranks! (Think of the Levite, whose conduct was far from irreproachable.) Then they shed crocodile tears when it turned out that they had gone too far in their lust for revenge. Finally, they sought a disgraceful remedy for the problem. They did not have the courage to admit that they had been too hasty and hot-headed in swearing an oath not to let their daughters marry Benjaminites.

All of this happened at the *beginning* of the period of the judges, when Phinehas was still alive (see 20:28). Thus we see clearly that the groundwork had already been laid for the later apostasy. Self-righteousness, insensitivity to sin, and superficial formalism never bear good fruit.

---

*Because King Saul was from Gibeah, we can well understand his eagerness to defend Jabesh-gilead (I Sam. 11). Many of the women of the tribe of Benjamin came from there.

4. Deborah's Song

Psalms outside the book of Psalms. If we are to understand the book of Judges properly, we must focus attention on a few of its other passages. One is Deborah's song. It's a shame that we don't sing the Old Testament psalms not included in the book of Psalms! These songs, unlike the 150 songs in the book of Psalms, have rarely been included in hymnbooks.

The beauty of Deborah's song cannot be denied. The first part (5:1-11) speaks repeatedly of Yahweh (the LORD) and Israel. In verses 3 and 5, the two are bound together in a kind of refrain: "The LORD, the God of Israel." This is the doctrine animating the song of Deborah: *Yahweh* fights for Israel, but *Israel* must also fight for Yahweh.

Echoes of Moses. The beginning of this song reminds us of Moses' benediction in Deuteronomy 33, where the Lord is also described as the God of Sinai. The Lord follows the same path to come to the help of His people as He followed in days of old.

Yet Israel is not to be a passive observer of this deliverance: the tribes must come "to the help of the LORD" (5:23). Meroz, a town that did not respond to the call for mobilization, is cursed. Reuben is spoken of in sarcastic terms because of his "great searching of heart." Like Manasseh (Gilead), Dan and Asher, Reuben was so cowardly as to stay home on the day of battle.

Jael is blessed in imaginative language for her courage. Deborah's song also gives us a glimpse of the mother of Sisera—Sisera is the captain who died at Jael's hand—as she waits in vain for her son. In the final verse, we hear the theme of the whole song reiterated:

> So perish all thine enemies, O LORD!

> But thy friends be like the sun as he rises in his might (5:31; see Matt. 13:43; 17:1ff; Rev. 1:16).

5. Gideon's Attempt at Reformation

Gideon's calling. In Gideon's days, Israel faced the attacks of nomads. That's why Gideon was busy threshing wheat in the wine press. There, he hoped, he would escape detection.

A prophet had already arisen to remind the people how God had delivered them in the past. Yahweh had led His people out of Egypt, but He forbade them to worship idols. Because the Israelites did not listen to the prophet, their situation grew more and more perilous.

It may be that Gideon knew what the prophet had been saying, for when the angel of the LORD appeared to him and said, "The LORD is with you, you mighty man of valor," Gideon was quick to point out that the Lord had always been able to deliver Israel *in the past.* If the Lord would be with him now, wonders such as those that occurred during the time of the exodus might be possible again. "But now the Lord has cast us off," Gideon complained, "and given us into the hand of Midian" (6:11ff).

The angel encouraged him. "Go to this might of yours and deliver Israel from the hand of Midian." Gideon could not yet bring himself to believe, and therefore he asked for a sign. The angel of the LORD responded by having Gideon place some food on a rock. He then touched the food with the tip of his staff. Fire erupted from the rock, consuming the food, and the angel disappeared.

Reformation at home. Before Gideon could assume the role of deliverer, he had to prove his willingness to serve the Lord fully. The reformation would have to begin in his own family's household. He was ordered to build an altar to the Lord and sacrifice on it "the second bull seven years old." This way of referring to the animal was typical among farmers of that era.

The age of the bull (seven years) may have had something to do with the fact that the Israelites had been oppressed by the Midianites for seven years. (The people in the ancient Near East were more sensitive to such symbolism than we are.) After seven years, the Israelites would finally start serving the Lord again.

We read that Gideon had to take down the altar and the sacred pole on his own family's homestead! Even in the "best" of families, then, the degeneration had gone a long way.

Signs from God. Gideon mobilized various tribes for battle, but he himself was not yet ready to proceed. He asked for signs from God and received them. The fleece he had left on the ground overnight was wet in the morning when everything else was dry, and the next morning it was dry when everything else was wet (6:36ff).

The Lord also encouraged Gideon by way of a spying expedition: Gideon heard that one of the Midianites had a dream in which the Midianites were defeated (7:9-14). In this dream, a cake of barley bread possessing tremendous power came rolling into the valley where the Midianites were camped. Barley bread, which is the food of the poor, was an apt symbol for Israel. This "sign" gave Gideon an idea for a plan of attack.

A night attack. At the Lord's command, Gideon first divided his men into two groups on the basis of how they drank at a stream. He sent the larger group home. No one could later proclaim that the Israelites had been saved by their own might. There was to be no room for human boasting (see 7:2).

In the end Gideon had only 300 men at his command. By blowing trumpets, shouting, and breaking jars during a night attack, they frightened the Midianites into thinking that they were being attacked by a huge army. Once the Midianites panicked, Gideon and his men were able to win a resounding victory.

Gideon's failure. When we go on to read chapter 8 of Judges, we see that there was a decline in Gideon's life. He could not resist showing off the kings he had captured. Although he refused to be crowned king, he was involved in a transgression of the second commandment; Scripture calls it "playing the harlot" (8:27; see also Rev. 2:14, 20). Earlier we saw what happened to Gideon's son Abimelech and the rest of the family after Gideon's death. There was fratricide, idolatry and revolution—the same old story of apostasy that we read again and again in Judges.

Gideon's age cried out for the *faithful* Judge and Deliverer Jesus Christ, who completes everything He undertakes. As Lord's Day 12 of the Heidelberg Catechism points out, Christ guards and safeguards the freedom He has won for us. That's just where the judges failed: they could not preserve the safety and freedom they gained for Israel. Only Christ can do so.

6. Jephthah and His Vow

Jephthah's daughter. Much has been written about the sacrifice of Jephthah's daughter. Because of a foolish vow, Jephthah felt bound to offer his daughter, his only child, as a burnt offering to the Lord.

Some scholars believe that such a sacrifice did indeed

take place, for the Bible speaks of a *burnt offering* (11:31). Others maintain that this term must not be taken literally. They argue that Jephthah's daughter "bewailed her virginity," sacrificing herself by never marrying. Like any other girl, she would like to have gotten married, but she did not (see 11:37-9). The sacrifice, then, would be her abstinence from marriage.

A weak instrument. The history lesson directed by Jephthah toward the Ammonites makes it clear that he was at home in "the Bible." Although he had grown up outside the covenant (11:2) and had not gotten the best impression of "the church," Jephthah chose God's people to be his own people and familiarized himself with the Lord's ways with Israel. Surely he knew how Abraham took Isaac up on Mount Moriah to sacrifice him to the Lord. He must also have been aware that the Israelites had been commanded not to make burnt offerings of their children, as the Canaanites sometimes did. Hence it is not likely that Jephthah, as a judge, would set a horrible heathen example by actually sacrificing his own daughter.

We must bear in mind that Samuel makes a favorable reference to Jephthah (I Sam. 12:11), and that another such reference occurs in the New Testament (Heb. 11:32). Jephthah was an instrument of deliverance in God's hand. Even though he was only a weak instrument, he was still a shadow pointing ahead to the Christ.

7. Samson and the Philistines

An office-bearer. Samson, too, was a shadow of what Christ would be. If we read his "story" in the light of the values of the modern world, we are inclined to think of him as some sort of "Tarzan." Scripture speaks of him, however, as a "Nazirite to God," a deliverer (13:5), and a judge (15:20).

It has been suggested that although Samson is one of the "heroes of faith" mentioned in Hebrews 11, his inclusion could not be based on what we learn about him in Judges. This line of reasoning overstates the case. Certainly there are dark shadows across Samson's life. Yet time and again we see how the invincible *grace* of the Lord is at work in the life of this amazing man, using him and forcing him down the pathway of faith.

It is precisely because the office-bearer Samson is such a sinner that his life cries out for Christ. Yet the gracious fact stands: the strange figure of Samson in his office of judge is a foreshadowing—albeit a weak one—of the One who not only *began* Israel's deliverance but will carry it through by delivering the Church and securing a wonderful future for her.

Birth announcement. In chapter 13 we are told how Samson's birth was announced to his parents. As we read this story, we must remember that there is nothing wrong with enjoying a Bible story as a story. We can savor the fine descriptions of Samson's father and mother.

The mother makes a strong impression on us as the angel, whom she takes for a prophet, appears to her. Her husband is most inquisitive when he hears her story. He wants to make the acquaintance of this "man of God," this prophet. His prayer is heard. The messenger tells him to prepare a burnt offering. Then, just as in the story of Gideon, flames erupt from the altar to consume the offering, and the angel vanishes.

When Samson's father finally realizes that it was the angel of the Lord, he is terrified. Won't he surely die now that he has seen the Lord? But his wife doesn't lose her senses. Why would the Lord give them such a revelation about the son to be born if He planned to kill them?

The name *Samson* means *little sun.* (*Shemesh* is the Hebrew word for *sun*. The town of Beth-shemesh—the name means *house of the sun*—was close to Zorah, Samson's birthplace.) It may be that Samson's mother—the woman is again the important figure—gave him this name because she expected that the sun of salvation would now shine on Israel.

The Philistines. In those days the Philistines dominated the Israelites and inflicted a number of grave defeats upon them. Even the ark of the covenant fell into enemy hands at one point.

These Philistines were actually western immigrants who may have come originally from Crete (see Amos 9:7). Naturally, they had already adapted somewhat to their Near Eastern environment, but they retained parts of their earlier culture. This was evident in their military style. When we read about the weapons and conduct of the Philistine giant Goliath, we are reminded of the stories recorded by the Greek poet Homer.

The god of the Philistines was Dagon. Earlier scholars argued that this god was half man and half fish. (The Hebrew word *dag* means *fish*.) More recently it has come to light that the name *Dagon* has something to do with the word *dagan*, which means *grain*. Thus Dagon must have been a Babylonian agricultural god whom the Philistines adopted as their own.

Betrayed by his brothers. In his first action against the Philistines, Samson attacks the "blessings of Dagon" by setting fire to the Philistines' standing grain (15:5). Judges 14 gives us the background to this event. Although we can hardly grant all of Samson's exploits our approval, we must not lose sight of the fact that he was driven by the Spirit, as the Bible expressly informs us (13:25).

When Samson was forced to hide out in the territory of Judah—he himself was of the tribe of Dan—the men of Judah were all too willing to hand the troublesome fugitive over to the Philistines. It appeared that the Israelites regarded resistance to the Philistines as hopeless. Thus Samson was betrayed by his own brothers. There was little solidarity or communion of the saints to be found among the Israelites.

The jawbone of an ass. At that very moment, however, the Spirit led Samson to exercise his office of deliverer. At Ramath-lehi he broke free of his bonds and killed a thousand men with the jawbone of an ass (see also Josh. 23:10).

Samson's song of triumph includes a pun that cannot be properly reproduced in our language, for he plays on a Hebrew word that can mean either *donkey* (ass) or *heap.* James Moffatt has translated the first two lines of Samson's song as follows:

> With the jawbone of an ass
> I have piled them in a mass!

Compare the translation in the New English Bible:

> With the jawbone of an ass
> I have flayed them like asses;
> With the jawbone of an ass,
> I have slain a thousand men (15:16).

After the triumph, we see just how small and childlike this "Tarzan" is. He is thirsty, and there is no water. In a prayer Samson admits that the Lord is the one responsible for delivering the Israelites. He now asks God to save him in his present predicament. Isn't that an expression of faith, the faith of a child? The Lord gives him water. Samson therefore calls the newly created spring the "spring of the caller." We are reminded of Psalm 110:

> He will execute judgment among the nations.
> He will drink from the brook by the way;
> therefore he will lift up his head (vs. 6,7).

Delilah. And then there is the story of Samson and Delilah. Samson certainly had to pay a heavy price for the sin of taking his office too lightly (16:4ff). But at the end of his life, when his hair had grown back, he was once more a Nazirite and judge and deliverer.

The "little sun" could no longer see, for the Philistines had gouged out his eyes. But the Lord gave him the strength to put a sudden, unexpected end to the shouts of "Praise Dagon!" The ruins of Dagon's temple became a monument honoring Yahweh.

Samson's burial. Samson's family dared to dig his body out of the ruins for a proper burial, which was an indication that Israel was again becoming aware of its obligations to the Lord. We see a new day dawning: the fallen hero mobilizes the dispirited Israelites. Later Samuel was to inflict a decisive defeat on the Philistines (see I Sam. 7).

But what do all these violent deeds have to do with Christ? For one thing, they remind us that Christ will make His enemies feel His wrath. Samson has shown us something of what this means. Christ completes the work begun by the judges, who faltered again and again. He is the beginning and the end of our deliverance. He has finished what He set out to do.

Ruth

1. Under the Lord's Wings

Another appendix to Judges. The book of Ruth begins with the words: "In the days when the judges ruled . . . . " We saw that the book of Judges had two appendixes containing stories typical of the times. In chapters 17 and 18 we read about Micah and his priest, while chapters 19-21 describe the shameful events in Gibeah, where the sin of Sodom had come into vogue, and the punishment of Benjamin for taking Gibeah's side when the evil led to a conflict. The second appendix, especially, shows us just how dark Israel's middle ages were.

But there is more to be said about the time of the judges. The book of Ruth forms what we might call a *third* appendix to the book of Judges. The light that breaks through in the story of Ruth contrasts sharply with the darkness in the tales about Micah and Gibeah.

A chapter of redemptive history. We need not shrink from admitting that the book of Ruth reads like a novel. There is suspense built into this story, which has a happy ending. It illustrates once more how much beauty there is to be found in Scripture.

Many centuries have passed since the events described in the book of Ruth. Yet the characters in the book don't seem at all remote: Naomi, with her sharp tongue; Ruth, who apparently needed to be "evangelized" but submitted more than anyone else to the yoke of the Kingdom; and Boaz, the farmer of few words, a man of solid, reliable character.

We must not forget, however, that the book of Ruth is part of the Bible. It is not just an idyllic tale about an agricultural village in the distant past; it falls within the framework of redemptive history. In this book, the Lord shows us how He was at work in the dark time of the judges when there was no king in Israel, how He was preparing the way for the birth of a king after God's own heart.

The book of Ruth ends with *David*. There was no king in Israel, and everyone did what was right in his own eyes. Yet the Lord was busy fulfilling the promise of Genesis 3:15: King Jesus was on the way! The Moabite Ruth joins the Canaanites Tamar and Rahab: all three are in Christ's line of descent (see Matt. 1:5).

The triumph of grace. What was a *Moabite* doing in Israel? Moab has a poor reputation in redemptive history. Moab was originally born out of incest (Gen. 19:31ff). At Baal-peor Moab had proved to be a deadly danger to Israel: Moabite women led the Israelites into harlotry and apostasy (Num. 25). That's why the law stipulated that there were to be no Moabites present at the assembly of the Lord.

The Moabites were related to the Israelites by blood. For this reason the Lord took steps to make sure that the Israelites would stay away from the Moabites, who served the god Chemosh in shameless sensuality (Deut. 23:3). Yet,

Ruth was one of the daughters of Moab.

The story of Ruth represents a wonderful triumph of God's grace. Pentecost colors come through strongly in this book, which the Jews customarily read aloud in the synagogue when they hold their Feast of Pentecost.

Ruth's decision. Ruth, it appears, was a straightforward woman, guileless as a dove. In other words, she was not a complicated personality seeking to attain her goals through scheming and plotting. When she chose for Yahweh and denied Chemosh, she did so with her whole heart.

She made her choice against Naomi's advice; Naomi (whose name means *pleasant* or *charming*) was not about to make the path to the land of Yahweh an easy one for Ruth to follow. On the contrary, she advised her two widowed daughters-in-law to return to their own people, expressing the hope that the Lord would be with them and would give them "rest" (i.e. fullness of life) in a second marriage (1:8-9). What future would there be in Israel for a marriageable Moabite woman? (1:11ff). Who would want to marry a foreigner who had fallen on hard times—and a Moabite at that? Furthermore, it seemed that the Lord had turned against Naomi; everything went wrong for her.

Orpah listened to these arguments and returned to her own people, but Ruth insisted on staying at Naomi's side. With an oath and a confession of her faith, she emphasized her determination that Naomi's people should henceforth be her people.

Bitterness and perseverance. Once they got back to Bethlehem—the name of the town means *place of food*—Naomi made it more difficult and painful for Ruth by declaring that she went away *full* but the Lord brought her back *empty*. Charming Naomi had become Mara, i.e. bitterness.

But did Naomi really come back empty? She did have

Ruth with her as a determined servant of the Lord. Wasn't Naomi's sarcasm a bitter denial of the faithfulness of Ruth?

The Moabite woman didn't let Naomi's harsh words drive her from the pathway of faith she had chosen. We stand amazed at her determined perseverance; we are touched by it. Despite her difficult circumstances, Ruth chose to live by the law of Yahweh, even in such practical, down-to-earth matters as seeking food.

The Lord had stipulated that widows, orphans, foreigners, and poor people must be allowed to glean what had been left behind during the harvest. The harvesters were to see to it that there was a little left over (Lev. 19:9). Ruth made use of this provision of the law, and thus she "happened" to be gleaning in the fields of Boaz (2:1ff).

Law and blessing. Keeping the law in daily life leads to blessing. Ruth was not above the lowly task of following the harvesters to glean whatever they might have left. Of course this was not the most pleasant kind of work, for there was a definite danger of being molested by the laborers in the field (see 2:9).

Ruth did not draw any false conclusions from the deplorable behavior of certain boorish members of "the church." She did not say, as so many others have said, "If that's what the church is all about, I want nothing to do with it." Ruth had chosen first and foremost for the Lord of the church—and she stuck by her choice. What Boaz said about her was true: she had indeed found refuge under the Lord's wings. She sought the protection of those wings in her life's struggle. Therefore the grace of the Lord was present in her life.

2. Under the Wings of Boaz

Redemption laws. Boaz, whose name means *strength*, was a kinsman of Naomi. You recall that God's law provided means of assistance for an impoverished family in danger of dying out. Leviticus 25 raised the possibility of "redeeming" the land: the nearest blood relative would buy back the land that the poor family had been forced to sell and would then restore it to the family. Deuteronomy 25 lays down the provisions for levirate marriage: if a man died childless, his brother was to marry his wife. Their first-born son would be regarded as the son and heir of the dead brother, which would assure the continuation of his line in Israel. The man who married such a woman without children was called the liberator or deliverer or redeemer (*goel*), for he built up the house of his brother.

The custom of levirate marriage was already a factor in the story of Tamar (Gen. 38), which took place long before the law governing such situations was given to Israel (Deut. 25:5-10). This custom is to be found among other ancient peoples as well, and also among some of the tribes of modern Africa.

A "love story." Chapter 3 of the book of Ruth must be read against this background. Of course Naomi, who was as cunning as a serpent and was well aware of what was going on in Ruth's heart, played an important role in this story. But Ruth was not someone to get involved in a *plot*. In this "love story," she followed the law of the Lord. It was her obedience to the law that sent her to the threshing floor of Boaz.

When Ruth encountered Boaz, she held him to his own words. Boaz had said that she had come to find refuge under *the Lord's wings*. That memorable night Ruth asked Boaz, as the redeemer, to take her under the protection of *his wings*. (The same Hebrew word is used as in 2:12, but most English translations render it as *skirt* in 3:9.) She appealed to him as the kinsman to whom the levirate law applied.

Because she had come under the protection of the Lord's wings, Ruth declared, Boaz should spread his wings over her by making her his wife (see also Ezek. 16:8). Here, too, the Lord uses human means to protect His people. Safety is to be sought in obedience to the law.

When we read between the lines, we sense that Boaz and Ruth were already head over heels in love with each other. But the bond between them was not just purely "natural." They found each other in the Lord.

Boaz was amazed that Ruth did not use the usual feminine methods to catch her man but sought a solution to her problem in the *levirate law*, even though Boaz was apparently a good deal older than she was (see 3:10). Respect for the levirate law made Boaz wait before marrying Ruth. Another kinsman, who would have prior claim to her according to the levirate law, first had to be asked whether he wished to exercise his right to marry Ruth.

When Ruth left, she was given six measures of barley for Naomi. Those measures of barley symbolized their situation. Everything would turn out all right in the end. The number seven, symbolizing the end of waiting, was near.

Faith's pathway. Chapter 4 presents the denouement of this drama. The people at the city gate gave their approval. One of the elders delivered a speech sprinkled with references to Israel's national history: Rachel, Leah, and even Tamar were mentioned (4:11-12).

At issue in the story of Tamar was the same problem, the problem that the levirate law was meant to deal with. The Lord had certainly blessed the descendants of Judah and Tamar! Surely there was some comfort in this for Ruth, the Moabite. Because the members of the tribe of Judah were not of the "purest" descent, they were in no position to point the finger at a descendant of Moab.

We, who have a better perspective on these redemptive facts, can hear the gospel of God's free grace coming through here. The Moabite woman who clung tenaciously to faith's pathway is granted the honor of playing a role in the advent of the great Redeemer (*goel*) Jesus Christ. The doctrine that there is no salvation outside the Church is exemplified in her story.

Messianic warmth. The happy outcome also brought joy into the heart of Naomi. Life had not come to an end for her. Her bitterness gave way to a Messianic warmth that flooded her life.

What the book of Ruth shows us is love and fate under the blessing of the *covenant*; it shows us daily life in the service of the Lord, who fulfills His promises. In the days when the judges ruled, God's work proceeded. One day there would be a fresh growth. A lion would arise from the tribe of Judah—with Tamar and Ruth in His line of descent.

Index